Gwendolyn Burton holds back nothing in this profoundly beautiful and strongly supportive book for those in grief and those who love them—including friends and family eager for loved ones to "get over it" and "move on." Writing with both courage and candor, Gwendolyn honors the process, shock, and seasons of grief as she plots out concrete ways to honor the pain of loss and the gift of self care while moving forward with God to find life beyond sorrow. A lovely and hard-fought resource for reading, gifting, praying, and sharing, it shines light and hope on every page for a path that needs both.

—Patricia Raybon, author of *I Told the Mountain to Move*
and *The One Year® God's Great Blessings Devotional*

Patricia Raybon is an award-winning Colorado author, essayist, and novelist who writes stories of faith and mystery. Her debut 1920s mystery novel, *All That Is Secret*, is a Parade Magazine Fall 2021 "Mysteries We Love" selection and a Masterpiece on PBS "Best Mystery Books of 2021" selection "As Recommended by Bestselling Authors."

A remarkable work! Gwendolyn eloquently weaves her personal journey through grief with her full heart, her honesty, humility, and strength. *You Don't Know Just How I Feel* deconstructs society's stereotypes regarding the "appropriate" way to grieve and validates our unique and individual paths as we move through the process. Her compassion radiates through each page in the book. She gives us the tools to embrace our grief—without rules and without apology. Her use of personal life experience shows her humanity and care for those who are attempting to make sense of their journey through the darkness. This book is essential for those beginning their journey through grief, who are on the pathway of grief, and even for those who are supporting others during the grief process.

—Dr. Claudia Crosse-Wynn
Licensed professional counselor/certified addictions counselor

I count it an honor and a privilege to call Gwendolyn Burton a spiritual daughter and sister in the faith both privately and publicly. While Gwendolyn refers to me as her mentor and spiritual leader, Gwendolyn, in her own right and by her desire to strengthen and encourage others who are grieving and experiencing personal tragedy, has proven to be a mentor and leader in the area of living with grief. As Gwendolyn's pastor I have watched her walk through some difficult places on her journey, but none as painful as the grief and loss of her beautiful son Miles. Many people have endured great loss and tragedy in their lives, but not everyone is willing or able to bear their hearts and souls in such a way that encourages, strengthens, and instructs other grieving hearts to continue to live—that grief and joy can co-exist in the same space. When I picked up this book, I didn't put it down until I finished it. And although I cried at times, I also smiled; I grew and learned. And now because of *You Don't Know Just How I Feel*, I am informed, empowered, and better equipped as a pastor to help others who grieve. Thank you, Gwendolyn, for not giving up on yourself but staying the course and depositing your book, the people's book, into the earth.

—Pastor Anitha Jones, FHG1 Ministries
Author of *Beyond Your Breakdown to Your Breakthrough*,
Certified Christian life coach

You Don't Know Just How I Feel left me spellbound. I laughed out loud, cried, and rejoiced regarding God's healing power of "moving forward." The theme strewn throughout the fabric of this book. I felt like I was relaxing in Gwendolyn's living room with a cup of tea, speaking to a loving friend while reading this book. Suffering the tragic loss of my younger brother and then my mother eight weeks later shattered my world. Gwendolyn's illustrations, sharing, and guidance let me know that I wasn't alone in how I felt and that there was hope on the other side of my sorrow. This author has an intuitive knack for comforting readers with her wisdom, practical advice, and transparency. I found she offered those dealing with grief and loss an outstanding balance of godly encouragement and factual knowledge. This combination helps address our emotions, intellect, spirit, and physical. Whether you're grieving or not, you can trust Gwendolyn with your hurting heart.

—Katherine Hutchinson-Hayes, Ed.D.
Author, editor, educational consultant, biblical counselor

We held a family memorial a month or so after my brother passed away from cancer at only 56-years old. At the end of the service, a trickle of tears escalated into a torrent of grief and heaving sobs that I couldn't control. No one else was crying. I felt embarrassed, of course, and my wife sought to comfort me. There were no words for my feelings of abandonment or the bleak finality of it all. After reading Gwendolyn's book, I see that my outburst of grief was quite natural, if awkward and misunderstood in the moment.

Gwendolyn has reached into and through her own deep grief in losing Miles, AJ, and others in her life to bring us a vital and sensitive companion to our own grief, giving us the most beautiful insights into how to better bless and comfort others as we encounter theirs. I now have a list of at least twenty-two things I'll never say again to anyone experiencing such sorrow. Thank you, Gwendolyn, for so generously opening your heart to share your story and to give us a better way forward through this veil of tears.

—John Chisum, president, Nashville Christian Songwriters,
Author, self-empowerment coach

It is with immense pleasure to recommend and endorse Gwendolyn Burton's work, *You Don't Know Just How I Feel*. Gwendolyn bravely recounts her grief journey in the loss of her son. She shares her personal tragedy with detailed nuance. I highly encourage anyone who has experienced loss, or knows someone who has, to read this book. As a bereaved mother myself, I was taken by the raw truth of her journey and the recommendations and hope she offers after enduring such a horrendous loss. I am confident this book will be an inspiration to so many who are walking in her/our steps.

—Julie Henckel Hutchison, president
The Chelsea Hutchison Foundation

Gwendolyn Burton has one of the most powerful and amazing stories that I have ever heard. As the words leap off the pages, you will experience Gwendolyn's God-given empathy and compassion for others. This book will touch your mind, your heart, and your spirit. You will truly feel empowered to move forward.

—Jason Alan Robinson, IFBB pro athlete, CEO of JARFit,
CEO of Prodigy Performance Supplements

Gwendolyn Burton hits a home run in her debut book, *You Don't Know Just How I Feel*, reminding us all that life's transitions are experienced individually, but at the same time we all share the commonality of pain and loss that is ever present in our lives and unavoidable where there is love. Kudos for a job well done, for sharing your story, and for leading, enlightening, and instilling hope in the area of grief.

—Jennifer C. Robinson, Esquire
Managing attorney, Robinson & Associates Law Office

You Don't Know Just How I Feel

You
Don't Know
Just
How I Feel

HOPE FOR THE GRIEVING HEART

GWENDOLYN O. BURTON

FOREWORD BY CECIL MURPHEY, NEW YORK TIMES BESTSELLING AUTHOR

Published by Redemption Press, PO Box 427, Enumclaw, WA 98022.
Toll-Free (844) 2REDEEM (273-3336)

Contact And Follow Gwendolyn O. Burton
    Email: movingforwardwithgb@gmail.com
    Website: www.gwendolynoburton.com
    Facebook: @moving forward with gwendolyn burton
    Instagram:@gwendolynoburton

Redemption Press is honored to present this title in partnership with the author. The views expressed or implied in this work are those of the author. Redemption Press provides our imprint seal representing design excellence, creative content, and high-quality production.

The author has tried to recreate events, locales, and conversations from memories of them. In order to maintain their anonymity, in some instances the names of individuals, some identifying characteristics, and some details may have been changed, such as physical properties, occupations, and places of residence.

All Scripture quotations are from the Holy Bible, New International Version®, NIV®. Copyright © 1973, 1978, 1984, 2011 by Biblica, Inc.™ Used by permission of Zondervan. All rights reserved worldwide. www.zondervan.com The "NIV" and "New International Version" are trademarks registered in the United States Patent and Trademark Office by Biblica, Inc.™

ISBN 13: 978-1-64645-631-4 (Paperback)
978-1-64645-633-8 (ePub)
978-1-64645-632-1 (Mobi)

Library of Congress Catalog Card Number: 2022902744

Contents

Dedication

*Y*OU DON'T KNOW JUST *How I Feel: Hope for the Grieving Heart* is dedicated to my loved ones who are the inspiration for this book.

My beloved son Christopher "Miles" Burton, my guiding light, my north star, whose life and memory continues to fill my heart with love and courage to move forward. Miles, you're the rainbow that breaks through the clouds and gives me the promise of hope on the stormy days. You're forever loved and never forgotten, my beautiful, beloved child.

To my (beloved) cherished nephew, Alvin "AJ" Odoms Jr., only God could have known that four years to the day, you would join your cousin Miles in heaven. Each morning when we awake we hear the echo of your voice reminding us to have a *Lovely Day*.

Miles and AJ, we miss you both beyond measure. As we endeavor to move forward in life we find comfort and assurance knowing that you're present with the Lord, and we will see you again.

To my three unborn children who transitioned by miscarriage. Though I never held you in my arms, my heart holds you in a special, sacred place.

To my mother, Ora D. Odoms, and grandmother, Eva Ann Odoms, thank you for giving me a foundation of faith on which to stand, and for showing me the meaning of resilience in the face of adversity and loss. Your examples of courage, strength, and perseverance have encouraged and undergirded me on my journey.

I honor your memories with the words in this book.

About the Cover

THROUGHOUT HISTORY THE DOVE has held significant meaning and symbolism. For those who grieve and mourn, the dove symbolism can be comforting and uplifting. The dove is a representation of the Holy Spirit and has been associated with messages of encouragement, healing, hope, love, navigation, peace, light, and purity.

Each time your eyes rest on the cover of this book or you pick it up to read, I pray you're reminded of the timeless, comforting, and uplifting symbolism that the dove represents and offers. As you navigate your grief journey, may you be guided by the gentle presence and purity the Holy Spirit brings to comfort, to lighten your path, and to guide you at all times, especially during times of distress and weakness.

May you find hope and encouragement in the pages of this book to lead you toward healing for your broken heart, enabling you to embrace life with a renewed purpose. Finally, may God's love, and the love you share with your departed ones, bring you comfort and peace on the wings of a dove.

Foreword

THE MORNING AFTER MY wife died, our pastor, Owen Stepp, visited. He'd hardly been seated before he leaned forward. "What was Shirley's favorite Bible verse?"

"Nahum 1:7." I tried to quote it, but in my grief, I couldn't get the words straight.

Owen smiled. Then he asked, "What's your favorite memory of her?"

For several minutes, he asked questions about Shirley. The way he asked and the intensity he showed as he listened, was one of the most healing events of my early grieving period.

Because he asked good questions and listened, I knew he cared.

By contrast, a week after my wife died, a friend visited and said, "It's time to move on. You knew she was dying, so get over it."

I'm sure he felt he was helping me. I thought, If only you knew how much I hurt. After that, I learned to hide my pain, thinking others had moved on, so I needed to do the same.

Only my best friend, David Morgan, seemed to grasp my pain. He came by every week and listened. Like Owen, he made it clear that he cared.

I was a former pastor, author, and public speaker, and I assumed everyone expected me to be strong and beyond my loss. I suffered in silence, and months lapsed before I was able to get beyond the grieving.

As Gwendolyn Burton points out, we all grieve differently. In my case, I had done a lot of what I call pre-grieving. For almost two months before Shirley died, I struggled with losing my wife.

Nothing I could do would change the inevitable. Shirley had been in poor health for at least five years and was getting worse. Spinal stenosis and an advanced stage of kidney disease made it clear to both of us that she was dying.

It didn't hurt less when she died, but I didn't have to face the shock of losing her.

As I was reading Burton's manuscript, it amazed me that moments of grief unexpectedly hit me. At first, I wondered, What's wrong with me? It's been almost nine years since she died, and yet many times the sense of loss grabs me and I mourn again.

Gwendolyn Burton's words encouraged me to feel my pain. Hardly a day passes when I don't think about her or remember things we did together.

I'm grateful for the insightful words and personal accounts in this book.

Cecil Murphey

Introduction

No one is immune to grief. There are those amongst us today who have grieved deeply in the past, and there are those who are grieving deeply now and sadly. All of us will grieve at some time in the future.

—Lorraine Kember

WHEN YOUR WORLD SHATTERS, you spiral down a black hole as shock, devastation, and grief shred every part of you—heart, soul, and spirit—into mere fragments of who you were before. No part is left untouched as you're sucked into deep, agonizing darkness. It's impossible to emerge intact.

"Put him on the floor," the 911 operator told my husband over speakerphone. "The paramedics are on their way. Do you know CPR?"

My husband struggled to move twenty-six-year-old Miles from his bed to the floor.

"We're already doing it!" I screamed, holding the cell phone.

"Stay with me," she said. "Keep doing CPR."

"Where are the paramedics?" Placing my mouth over my son Miles's, I forced air into his lungs. "One. Two. Three. Four. Five."

My husband leaned over Miles's body and continued the chest compressions. Right hand over his left, he pressed, one-one thousand, two-one thousand, three-one thousand. . . .

I cried between breaths. "He's still not breathing!"

After what seemed like an eternity, she asked, "Is the door open? The EMTs are outside."

Paramedics and firefighters rushed in with bags and equipment flung over their shoulders. Three of them began attending to Miles while they peppered question after question at us in rapid succession.

"He was fine," I answered, my voice shaking with each word. "We had just talked to him about ten minutes before he went downstairs . . . My husband found him . . . No. No drug use. He has epilepsy."

While the first responders readied my son for the ambulance, I walked outside and paced back and forth in my front yard, praying, pleading, crying, "God, please help Miles!"

"He will breathe. He will live," I repeated in a shaky chant.

Forty-five minutes later, the paramedics rolled Miles out on a gurney, loaded him in the ambulance, and drove to the hospital.

By this time our pastors had arrived. "We'll drive you," they said. My husband and I sat in the back seat of the car, continuing to pray as we followed the ambulance to the hospital. Soon family and friends arrived and joined us in the waiting room.

After a while the doctor came in and pulled my husband and me aside. "I want to prepare you for what you'll see before we go into the room. He's connected to a lot of tubes and he's hooked up to a breathing machine."

I took a deep breath, exhaled, and braced myself. *I can handle the tubes and machines. They remind me that my child will be okay.*

Our pastors joined my husband and me as we followed the doctor. Miles was like a son to them. He would feel reassured and comforted knowing that they were there with him. I felt secure and fortified having them beside us as we walked silently down the hallway like warriors of strong faith.

I scanned the room. Miles lay hooked up to several monitors. Ventilator tubes connected to his mouth, his chest rose and fell in sync with the rhythmic hissing coming loud then soft from the machine.

Despite my resolve, I flinched, holding my breath and clenching my teeth. Alarm rushed through me as I gazed at his still body. I stood beside his bed and shuddered at the coldness of the room. "Mamma's here, baby," I whispered as I took his hand in mine.

In shock, I squinted, trying to process the image of Miles lying there. No, this can't be happening. How could a seizure cause this? My heart began to pound as a quiet fear came over me.

But I shook myself. I was in battle mode. I couldn't allow fear to enter any part of my mind. If there ever was a time *for unwavering faith,* that time was now. I believed God would heal Miles. I believed in the we-have-the-victory kind of faith. Victory was now. My faith was strong. I knew God would bring Miles through this.

"He seems to be getting better," I said. "His breathing—"

"The machine is breathing for him." The doctor touched my shoulder. "Once we take him off, his heart will stop."

I was fighting for, praying for my child with every part of my being. "No! That can't be! He's going to be all right—"

"He was without oxygen for too long. There is no brain activity."

Opening my mouth in silent protest, immense tension filled my body. I shook my head in disbelief. "Doctor," I said with all the faith, courage, and conviction I could muster, "I appreciate and respect your medical expertise, but I serve a God who is able to cause Miles to breathe when you take him off that machine." I took a deep breath. "I need you now, God."

"You'll need to sign this, allowing us to disconnect the ventilator," the doctor said gently as she handed me a clipboard and pen. "I'll give you time to say goodbye."

After she left, immediate family members edged into the room. One by one they gasped, shaking their heads in disbelief, slow streams of tears slipping down their cheeks. Then wails erupted the silence. "No, God. No. Not Miles. Please, no."

With overwhelming agony, their cries pierced my body while thoughts of Miles consumed me. My husband, Bob, and our pastors wrapped my precious family members in their arms and tried to comfort.

I lay down beside Miles. His bare chest rested against my body. I put my arms across him, feeling his chest against my upper body.

"Dear God," I pleaded, "please let his heart keep beating. Keep him breathing."

And they removed the ventilator. Miles never breathed again.

My world had shattered. The unimaginable had happened. Two weeks before his twenty-seventh birthday, my son Miles suffered a seizure in bed, most likely Sudden Unexpected Death in Epilepsy (SUDEP).

Miles's death wasn't my first experience with child loss. I'd heard heartbreaking words from doctors before when they had stood beside my bed and given me the news.

"I'm sorry, but . . . ," each had said.

During the early years of my marriage, I'd endured three miscarriages, the first at four months, the second at three, and the third at two, each one leaving me lost and alone. I silently grieved my unborn children. I waded through those turbulent years of child loss, slammed by waves of anxiety, fear, and heartache. Though I never gave birth to those precious babies, I loved each one dearly and carry them in my heart.

Imagine my ecstasy when I experienced the miracle of becoming the mother of two beloved sons, born three years apart. I had finally emerged from the loss and grief. Being a mother became the joy of my life. Love and pride for my sons gave my life meaning and purpose.

But now, years later, death arrived again, claiming another child of mine.

Lost in disbelief and engulfed by grief, I was unsure if I could survive the devastation of Miles's death. Nothing in life, not even the pain of my previous losses, could've prepared me for living with the grief that followed.

Devastated, mass confusion trapped me in a horrible nightmare. *How could this happen to my child?* For months afterward, when I sat on the couch, lay in bed, or wherever I was, I tried to shake myself, wake up, and snap out of my depression. But I couldn't.

How can I go on? How can I live with this excruciating pain? What is there to live for?

Losing Miles had forced me on a chaotic journey into unknown territory. For anyone who has experienced loss, adapting to the magnitude of changes sets us on a rollercoaster careening with unexpected and endless curves, dives, flips, and twists. We feel unsettled, afraid, helpless, and sometimes out of control. We cry, yell, plead, and ache, hoping to stop time and for our world to return to what it was before our loss.

Wait. Stop. He's no longer here.

She died.

How can I continue my daily activities as if nothing's happened?

Our silent screams are unheard by those around us as they buzz through their days, checking off tasks on their to-do lists, rushing to their next appointment.

Life around us remains the same, even though everything is now different for the person grieving. Our world, and the life we'd known, ended when our loved one died. We plant an emotional marker and begin measuring life, time, and events as *before* and *after* our loved one transitioned.

The struggle of learning to live each day without their presence, without seeing their smiling face, without hearing the tenor of their voice, without holding their hand, without feeling their touch, or not being able to include them in our daily activities slowly becomes reality. It's impossible to fully prepare for life without them.

We yearn for someone to understand and care about the struggles of living with our loved one's death. We long for hope to believe we can survive death's agony and for faith to accept that our life still has purpose and meaning.

We want to know that we are not alone.

That's why I wrote this book. This isn't a how-to manual with answers to grief's vast impacts and complexities. This book provides tips and suggestions for navigating common areas we encounter along the grief journey. This book, as a tool, shines light for you, dear reader, where you can find hope and support for living life after experiencing loss.

If someone you love has died, this book is for you. I designed short, digestible chapters to help you reflect and process through your own grief. Each chapter explores a relatable topic shared from my personal grief journey, as well as from mothers and fathers of child loss I've personally spoken with, and from others I've met online who live across the United States and have diverse experiences. These precious hearts have graciously allowed me to share their stories.

For readers who seek to understand how they can support someone living with the impact of loss, grief, and mourning, this book is also for you. Some chapters will provide you with deeper understanding and ways to facilitate tender discussions about grief and how to interact more effectively with gentle, supportive actions and words.

As we explore the reality of living with grief together, my prayer is that you will find comfort, hope, validation, and healing to help you move forward.

With hugs, hope, and healing,
Gwendolyn Burton

PART 1
The Reality of Grief

CHAPTER 1

The Reality of Grief

Give sorrow words; the grief that does not speak
whispers the o'er-fraught heart and bids it break.

—William Shakespeare, *Macbeth*

THE FALLACY OF CONCEALING our grief keeps us trapped, while the need to be heard screams in our heads.

Sitting in the breakroom, I overheard two coworkers discussing another coworker, whose mother had died months previously and was visibly grieving.

"Mourning is a personal matter that people should do privately," one coworker said. "It's a sad part of life that we go through, and we move on."

Though some may disparage our need to grieve openly, what the coworker failed to understand is that others' deep heartache and desperate need to share their sacred, grieving space with us does *not* move on. Perhaps that coworker had never experienced the loss of a loved one, or maybe she'd been uncomfortable seeing someone grieve. Whatever her reason, the lack of understanding mourning and grieving over someone we love reflects a mindset that encourages the larger community to be silent about what hurts them.

The Fallacy of Covering and Concealing

We shouldn't view mourning, which is the *outward expressions* of our loss, as an inconvenience that impedes upon society's dictates.

Dr. Alan D. Wolfelt, author, grief counselor, and founder and director of the Center for Loss and Life Transition, termed mourning as "grief gone public." When we cry, talk about our loved one, celebrate meaningful events, or share our feelings through art, music, or writing—these are only a few examples of mourning.

Just as there's no right or wrong way to mourn, we shouldn't feel shame about grieving. What we feel *inside*, emotions, thoughts, and turmoil, is something others can't see. Others can't determine, judge, or see our grief simply by whether we're crying or upset.

When a significant person in our life dies, it changes us. Forever. We'll never be the person we were before. For many who live with grief, the *truth* of our experience provokes us to question the established concepts of what *acceptable* mourning looks and feels like. We understand that society's predetermined norms don't reflect our journey. Rather, they attempt to put us in a one-size-fits-all package where everyone follows the same path.

Some people think grief is a temporary and unpleasant experience that disrupts our lives. We deal with it, get over it, and return to our normal selves. Non-grieving people might expect us to confine grieving and mourning to acceptable times, places, and reactions. But time passes, and we wrestle with intense emotions—some confusing, some familiar, some new, and all rooted in heartbreak.

But when we struggle to appear normal, grieving outside others' parameters of acceptable expectations, we actually disrespect ourselves in our own grieving process. Each person grieves differently and does not progress along the same path as someone else. To escape and protect ourselves from other people's judgment, we camouflage our hurt. What we don't know is that others whom we think are *grieving the right way* have also learned to do what we are doing—withdraw and conceal their pain in something else. Consider Anne's experience.

> "After my sister died, my family and friends thought I was okay," Anne said. "I'd lost my mom a few years earlier and the death of my only sister felt almost unbearable. I was hurting so badly and didn't believe I could talk to anyone about it. Other relatives and

friends seemed to be handling her death just fine, and I didn't want anyone to think there was something *wrong* with me.

"I began going on shopping sprees and traveling across the country—often flying twice monthly to a different city. Before long, my spending was out of control, I was maxing out my credit cards, and in financial trouble. Two years later, my nephew— my sister's only child—died and I delved deeper into spending money that I couldn't afford. About two years ago, I hit a wall and became almost broke financially.

"That forced me to face the truth that I was covering my grief and hiding from my pain. I knew I had to do something differently." Taking a deep breath, she continued, "I'm now on track to rebuilding myself financially, but you're the only person I've felt I could talk to about my grief."

Many people can relate to Anne's experience of covering and concealing grief. While she sought to soothe her pain through shopping and traveling, there are many other ways we seek to hide our pain when we feel we can't talk about grief or grieve without judgment.

For example, people develop bad habits with food, alcohol, drugs, or sex. Some escape through work, isolation, or getting involved in unhealthy relationships.

When we break the silence about grief, we feel less alone, less different, and learn to make choices that help us navigate through our journey without believing we must hide and deny the authenticity of our experience.

In early bereavement, when we focus our attention on making final arrangements and a steady flow of people check on us, we may appear to function well. Some might assume that once the funeral or memorial service is over and the public acknowledgments have concluded that the severity of our heartbreak subsides.

"You've made it through the hard part," they say.

"Stay strong."

The truth is our excruciating journey has barely begun.

Often that's when the shock waves of our life-altering storm crash in and shatter our emotions into pieces. Darkness engulfs us and we pray, "God, please let this be a bad dream—a nightmare I'll soon awaken from."

Time passes, but for many of us, the dark, thick fog doesn't lift, and we can't escape. An unimaginable sadness weighs on us so heavily that we struggle to do the basics, like move our feet, lift our bodies, or get dressed. Confusion and disbelief set in, and we question if we're disconnected from reality.

Is my loved one really gone?
How can I go on without them?
This has to be a mistake.
This can't be true.

Our emotions shift from numbness to overwhelm. We've never experienced such intense heartbreak and don't know if we can make it through the day. Generally we reserve this aspect of mourning for private conversations and discussion. But to avoid, deny, and ignore the complete nature of bereavement in the public arena paints an incomplete picture and keeps us locked in insecurity and fear.

When we open the door to communal discourse and dispel the misconceptions and false expectations, we make room for a more accurate narrative that increases our knowledge about life after the death of a loved one.

This is the beginning of our healing journey.

Misguided and Misinformed

"Follow these five steps," someone suggests.

"Repeat these positive affirmations every day, and you'll be okay."

"Just get out of the house and focus on something else."

Many misguided and misinformed people believe that there are *normal* steps and routines that, if followed, will catapult us out of our sorrow and back into our old selves.

But when our sadness remains, we believe something's wrong with *us*. Yet this is not true because there is no such thing as a *normal* way to grieve—only *common* responses and behavior that most people go through. But it's difficult to know what's considered a common response or behavior unless we talk about it.

Long before Miles died, I'd experienced significant deaths—my mother, grandmother, and close friends. I responded to each death differently, and I still have days when I miss them sorely. But none of those bereavements plunged me to the darkest depths of despair as my son's death did.

We parents expect that we'll die before our children—we believe it's the *right* order of things. When Miles passed, my world spun off its axis. The natural order of life spiraled out of balance, hurling me into an unknown universe. I couldn't imagine I would ever survive the unrelenting emotional, physical, mental, and spiritual agony I endured.

Over the months and years after Miles's death, I came to understand that other parents hurt as deeply as I did. I reached out and shared my distress, and they told of theirs.

"Will this excruciating pain ever end?" we asked each other.

Through mutual sharing, I learned that my suffering and questions weren't isolated or uncommon. My friends, some dear, and others I'd met after Miles's transition, told me the truth—that I'd feel worse before I moved to a place where my pain would soften, that years would pass, and I might still agonize over Miles's death.

During the first two years, I couldn't envision myself living without him. I could barely live for each day. I learned that I needed to give myself permission to mourn and allow myself the freedom to articulate my sorrow.

Perhaps the death of a loved one has someone carrying a heavy heart filled with silent pain. Grieving hearts may highlight their brokenness in a yearly acknowledgment on social media, commemorating Mother's Day, Father's Day, or birthdays—society's acceptable times to express our sorrow. Otherwise, grief remains unacknowledged.

I've watched others carry the weight of sadness and press through their days with appeasing smiles on their faces. I imagined some were hurting intensely and understood the unspoken reality of the agony they bore.

When we reach out, join hands, and walk beside others in the well of grief, we disrupt the cycles of isolation and abandonment and build a community of healing and support.

Embracing Our Journey

Living with grief shouldn't make us timid or apologetic about how we mourn or grieve. We must allow ourselves to fully embrace the process of mourning and grieving as we learn to live with our new loss. I remind myself not to deny, suppress, or try to escape the turbulent emotions, but to go deep within and embrace them by feeling, touching, wrestling, and interacting with them on each level, in each area and phase of life.

When we learn to walk through loss without avoidance, each of us determines which level to interact with our grief. While not the same as the stages of grief, there *is* a correlation with the emotions and reactions we experience during those stages and the level of permission we give ourselves to feel, experience, and work through those painful emotions. Will that interaction be a level of subtle acknowledgment or a deep, intimate, intense one?

Facing our deepest fears, asking difficult questions, and confronting all the emotional, mental, physical, and spiritual pain empowers us to move forward in those areas. During each grief phase, as we move through the days, weeks, months, and years, the fear of feeling different emotions resurfacing will fade, giving way to courage to freely grieve.

Don't be afraid when sadness, tears, or the pain of loss comes and sits with you, because love is manifesting itself. Be present with it, honor it, and let it guide you into healing. There is no fear in love.

As conversations with others who are also grieving broaden, a selective group introduces a myriad of experiences, and we begin to tear down the fears, comparisons, emotions, and inaccurate thinking that prevent love from being present in grief. When we understand that facing our grief doesn't mean we're weak, we realize that we are resilient, courageous, and human. This is how we empower ourselves and others to move forward in our grief and to mourn without shame.

Once we accept that we have loved deeply and are able to mourn deeply, we can embrace our journey. As difficult as this may be, when we walk together with compassion, knowledge, and truth, each of us *will* make it through the storm.

Moving Forward

Don't be afraid when sadness, tears, or the pain of loss comes to sit with you. That's love manifesting itself. Be present with it, honor it, and let it guide you into healing. There is no fear in love.

When present in grief, love becomes a conduit of healing to the grieving person. This loving support allows the bereaved to:

1. Feel accompanied, cared for, and supported in grief, not judged or abandoned.
2. Experience the freedom to grieve in their own way.
3. To begin the journey of healing and moving forward.

CHAPTER 2

What's Happening to Me?

Grief is not a disorder, a disease, or a sign of weakness. It is an emotional, physical, and spiritual necessity, the price you pay for love. The only cure for grief is to grieve.

—Rabbi Earl Grollman

THOUGH EACH OF US responds to grief differently, there are many common reactions that most people will experience. Some of these responses we will recognize, while others might seem unfamiliar. We might feel frightened and debilitated, defenseless and lost, distressed and confused because we are unaware of what's happening inside of us.

Common Grief Responses

A few months had passed since Mark and I had talked, and almost a year since his wife's death. We stood by his car in the grocery store parking lot, the afternoon sun beaming down on us.

Beads of sweat trickled down the side of Mark's face. "My mind is scattered all over the place. I can't sleep. Sometimes I walk into a room and can't remember why I'm there." He sighed, shaking his head in exasperation. "A few weeks ago, I left the water running in the sink all night and flooded the kitchen floor. I don't know what's happening to me. I'm just not myself. Sometimes I think I might be losing my mind."

I took his hand in mine, now four years on my grief journey, hoping to bring him a ray of comfort. "My friend, there's nothing *wrong* with you. That's common in grief."

Listed below are common physical, mental, and emotional responses we may experience that can help us understand how grief might manifest itself.

- Anger
- Anxiety
- Changes in appetite
- Despair
- Exasperation of current existing medical issues
- Excessive work or activities
- Fatigue
- Forgetful, difficulty concentrating, fogged thinking, confusion
- Guilt
- Headaches, body aches, shortness of breath, tightness in the throat

- Crying
- Denial
- Depression
- Helpless
- Lonely
- Numb
- Overwhelmed
- Preoccupied
- Restless, the inability to sleep, or wanting to sleep all the time
- Sad
- Shock
- Weight loss or gain
- Yearning

Perhaps some of us withdraw or lose interest in social activities we engaged in before our loss. "I don't want to be around anyone right now," my friend Louis had shared. "I just want to be alone."

I understood his need to self-isolate as he tried to process the death of his son, and I'd done the same thing. Before Miles transitioned, I frequently joined my friends for lunch dates or a movie. On other occasions, we'd shop, go on a day trip, or simply get together and talk. Afterward, I lost interest in most things I'd previously enjoyed and isolated myself from social activities.

I later came to understand that when we withdraw, it's not always a sign that we're in trouble. Sometimes we need time alone to work through the shock, pain, and devastation in private, and this provides the sacred space to begin that work.

The stressors of grief may disrupt our normal rhythms and reactions; however, our bodies are made to respond and adapt to those changes. When we recognize and understand the relationship between our individual responses to grief, we can eliminate the distress of thinking that there's something wrong with us or we're not *doing* grief right. We learn to understand and accept that we're grieving the way we were created to. And many of those common reactions and responses are characterized by what some people refer to as stages of grief.

Stages of Grief

Jackie and I had met earlier that week at the home of a mutual friend. We connected easily after learning that we'd both experienced losses in recent years.

"Would you like to get together for coffee later this week?" I asked.

"That would be great," she replied.

Now, sitting across the table from her in the corner of the coffee shop, we began sharing how we were dealing with our grief.

"Have you gone through all the stages of grief yet?" Jackie asked as she sipped her coffee and placed the cup on the table. "I've been trying to figure out which stage I'm in, because sometimes when I think I've finished one of them, I'll have *a day* and I feel like I've gone backward. I thought I'd be further along by now."

The death of someone we love can catapult us into a range of grief reactions. Psychiatrist Elisabeth Kübler-Ross developed her theory of the five stages of death as they relate to terminal illness and discussed them in her book *On Death and Dying*. Later, in their book *On Grief and Grieving,* Dr. Kübler-Ross, along with grief expert David Kessler, revised these stages and called them the five stages of grief. That theory became an accepted model for how we process grief. Other professionals suggest that five stages don't sufficiently address the culture, personal dimension, or environment in which we experience and express grief. Various researchers theorize as many as twelve, which demonstrates there isn't a universal checklist or formula for progressing through grief.

A summary of the five-stage model provides basic insight when considering emotions mourners might experience. Countless people mistakenly interpret those five stages to be linear, and that after they've progressed through the stages, grievers are healed. However, the stages don't follow an order, not everyone experiences each stage—we may experience all or some. Mourners can move back and forth between the stages. There isn't a set timeframe, and each stage can last minutes, hours, weeks, or months.

The Five-Stage Model

1. Denial.

For many people, this is often the first reaction to loss. Denial is a natural coping mechanism that gives us time to understand and process our sudden situation. We're often in a state of shock, disbelief, and our feelings numbed. This stage slows down the pace of grief so that we're able to handle it. During this stage, we may repeat statements like:

"This can't be true."

"He can't be gone."

"She's coming home soon."

2. Anger.

As we move out of denial, sometimes suppressed emotions surface. Although feeling angry is normal, some people might insist this isn't a stage they experience. For most of us, allowing ourselves to feel anger is necessary for progressing toward healing. Sometimes guilty feelings accompany anger and may be expressed in remarks like these:

"If only I'd driven him there."

"If she hadn't gone to that party, this wouldn't have happened."

"God, why . . .?"

3. Bargaining.

During this stage, we may feel helpless and desperate. We yearn to wake up and find that we've been dreaming. We linger in the past, trying to make things right. "What if," "If only" and bargaining dialogue are common.

"God, I'll do this if you'll only take away this pain."

"God, let this be a dream and I'll do anything you want."

4. Depression.

As the initial fog lifts and we become present with our loss, many of us enter into deep grief. Overwhelming sadness and emptiness consume us. We withdraw and isolate ourselves. Mental health professionals stress that this isn't a sign of clinical depression, but a natural response to grief. The full weight of loss rests on us and we tell ourselves:

"I can't go on without my loved one."

"How can the world keep going when my loved one isn't here?"

"There's nothing to look forward to."

5. Acceptance.

Coming to accept loss is normally a gradual process. That doesn't mean we're fine or don't feel any pain, but we've arrived at a place of not resisting the reality that our loved one died. We learn to live day-by-day, adapt, adjust, grow, reconnect with others, and transform our lives. We start believing in the possibility of living life again.

In his book *Finding Meaning: The Sixth Stage of Grief*, grief expert David Kessler adds a sixth stage, personal knowledge from experiencing the death of his son.

6. Finding Meaning.

This final stage encourages grievers to find meaning that transforms grief into a more peaceful and hopeful experience. We learn to move forward by honoring and remembering our loved ones in meaningful ways, in order to facilitate moving away from suffering, and toward meaning.

Understanding these stages help those who are grieving, and those who support grieving people, acknowledge the magnitude of emotional changes mourners experience. Although there are similarities, no two people will follow the same path and, therefore, we shouldn't compare how one person grieves to anyone else. Much of what we feel within our unique grieving process is natural, which helps us find solace in affirming those emotions while navigating through grief.

In the early years after loss, we can feel we'll never progress beyond the brutal assault of emotional responses, and chaotic stages. We can find hope in another's journey when we accept that the capacity to bounce back and return to a place of emotional and physical calm is innate in each of us, even after the most devastating losses.

Moving Forward

The stages of grief don't follow an order, and not everyone experiences each stage—we may experience all or some. Mourners can move back and forth between the stages. There isn't a set timeframe, and each stage can last minutes, hours, weeks, or months. Experiencing one or more of the stages is evidence that you're progressing on your grief journey. Identifying and understanding our grief emotions empowers us to work with and through them and not run from them.

CHAPTER 3

"I Know Just How You Feel"

*The friend who can be silent with us in a moment of despair
or confusion, who can stay with us in an hour of grief
and bereavement, who can tolerate not knowing . . . not
healing, not curing . . . that is a friend who cares.*

—Henri Nouwen

MONIQUE AND I SAT in her parked car as she shared details of the pain others had unknowingly inflicted when they offered condolences. Days earlier, she'd suffered a devastating death and was trying to process the shock and gravity of it. It had been four years since Miles had died and I'd begun the grief journey she was now starting. I said nothing, only listened. As I watched her expressions, I sensed something more was troubling my friend.

Monique closed her eyes and spoke slowly. A deliberate pause after each of her next few words charged the atmosphere. She gripped her fist, fighting to maintain composure. I knew whatever Monique was about to say had pushed her to a place of painstaking anger that couldn't be restrained. Then her frustration exploded.

"If one more person tells me they know exactly how I feel, or asks what happened, or tells me my brother's in a better place, I'm going to go off on them!"

Don't Placate Me

I'd heard similar woes from others who'd experienced the passing of a loved one. Perhaps you've heard them and felt frustrated too.

Because it's often difficult to know what to say, condolences and sympathy from well-meaning family and friends might feel insensitive, rather than comforting and supportive.

I've been on both sides of that delicate interaction. In the past, I've been guilty of saying sympathetic words and expressions that may have caused a bereaved loved one or acquaintance to feel worse. And well-meaning people also offered sympathy during my bereavement that felt inappropriate and discrepant.

"You're strong, you will make it through this," some had said.

At that time I was devastated by my son's death, and the idea that I could make it through this because I was a strong person seemed to minimize the enormity of my pain.

This statement made me feel as if I were encased in a suit of armor and nothing could push through its exterior to weaken me. Yet my insides were like egg shells, ready to crack into a thousand pieces.

For most of us, knowing what to say to a grieving person doesn't come naturally. There are not any *perfect* healing words or soothing scripts to recite. Many sympathetic expressions and clichés are rooted and passed down through customs, cultures, institutions, and within communities of faith. We tend to repeat what we've heard others say. And, without understanding the impact of those words or phrases, this repetition often promotes a continuous valley of unknowingly inducing deep wounds against the grieving person.

Navigating the emotional minefield of sympathetic expressions can be painful and disparaging for the grieving person. Often they feel sad and hurt at such words and say nothing about the affront. Withdrawing, they remain silent as they process the words they've heard. Often the grieving resist drawing even more attention to their pain and, like my friend Monique, the brokenhearted are left empty and unserved.

And the well-intentioned sympathizer is unaware of the resulting harm their sympathy and words caused. We all respond differently in how we show support and react toward grieving people.

Sympathy, Empathy, and Compassion in Loss

Sympathy, empathy, and compassion are often used interchangeably and often misunderstood; however, while related to the family of support, each term shares a different meaning and each has a specific use. When we understand the difference of each expression, our response to those who hurt can have a greater impact.

Someone described sympathy as "being sorry their feet hurt" and empathy as "walking a mile in somebody else's moccasins." Compassion implies that in addition to seeing yourself in another's shoes or relating to them, you also have a deep desire to help or act on their behalf.

Sympathy

Sympathy is an external response with detached emotions characterized by general actions that let someone know you're thinking about them, and is often the polite or expected thing to do. Most people extend common condolences when someone dies. We visit and call, send cards and flowers, and give donations and bring over meals. When we sympathize with others, we're sorry for what they're going through, regardless of whether we've experienced the same situation. At best, we can only imagine what it feels like, and we can't know what their grief journey is truly like.

Empathy

Empathy listens to someone's deepest suffering without judgment or wanting to rush them or make them feel better or fix them or their situation. Empathy is experienced when we learn to eliminate or set our own feelings aside and focus on the griever's experience. *Sharing* another's feelings and *understanding* them allow us to connect with their sorrow, meeting people where they are. We feel sad *with* someone as we identify with the situation. Our goal is to understand the depth of what they feel about their loss. When we can imagine what it might be like to experience their pain as our own, we build awareness.

I've been empathetic for most of my life. Personal traumatic experiences have taught me empathy. Through those shared experiences,

I learned to walk alongside hurting people and share their deep emotional anguish with compassion.

Conversely, empathy can become unhealthy when we take on someone else's pain *as our own* and carry it within ourselves. It's difficult to provide support and understanding to grieving people when we allow ourselves to assume their pain; we become exhausted, overwhelmed, or sacrifice our own well-being.

With that understanding, living with grief has expanded my capacity for empathy, which is a learned behavior, enabling us to show up and be present for family and friends when they need us most. David Kessler says that "to feel too much is dangerous and to feel too little is tragic." That's empathy to an extreme level. But compassion. Compassion is much different.

Compassion

Compassion shows care, love, and kindness when we see people in pain. I've watched stories on television and have known people who've suffered devastation and loss from natural disasters, accidents, or gun violence. Learning of someone's personal loss sparked my compassion because I was concerned about their suffering. *What can I do to express my concern and support?* I was sad for the pain they endured and would often provide emotional and other support.

Compassion requires a deeper level of commitment and service than empathy does, and provides heartfelt empathy with a servant's heart. Being willing or able to step outside of ourselves and our personal agendas and bias to meet the needs or ease the suffering of others is a compassionate act. Showing that we care and are concerned about the condition of others. Responding with words, actions, or deeds, big or small, allows us to give of ourselves and our resources in a way that changes another's state or condition in grief.

By building awareness that promotes a more compassionate environment, our sensitive actions help us set intentions that create a safe space for the grieving. Yet when sympathetic expressions are spun in an inconsiderate way, sometimes our efforts to meet people in their grief become hurtful. Conversely, some people are able to connect and support the bereaved comfortably when they share a common grief experience. Through compassion, we care about people who are hurting and we value the bond of connecting with them. We bear witness with other people's grief and reach out to connect with them, without internalizing their pain.

When Sympathy Turns Painful

I haven't always addressed sensitive grief issues. During a time when the bereaved are emotionally fragile, such conversations and insensitivities may trigger painful emotions, memories, and cause deep pain and resentment.

Through talking about grief with others, I've understood that people share in private what they're uncomfortable saying in public or to someone they know personally. Many people have shared that when friends and loved ones crossed emotional boundaries with statements or questions, they felt traumatized.

Similarly, many grievers have admitted that during their mourning some common clichés and words of sympathy felt improper and poorly suited. Often these kinds of words and phrases might make the bereaved feel judged or scrutinized. From my own experience, I have learned to not judge their emotions or grief journey because it's not helpful and is often damaging.

A bereaved acquaintance shared that she stopped going to church and distanced herself from certain friends because she dreaded hearing their expressions.

"He's in a better place."

"God doesn't put more on you than you can bear."

"God doesn't make mistakes."

"His work here was done."

"He wouldn't want you to be sad."

"Be glad you had them as long as you did."

While I believe these expressions are true, when my own grief was raw, hearing these words caused more pain than comfort. It's human nature for people to question or talk about the details and trauma of a person's passing; yet it's often better to develop insight so we can respect the bereaved person's decision to share information—only if *they* choose. And sometimes this comes through shared experiences.

Empathy through Shared Experience

Some experiences, like the death of a child, only a parent who has experienced that loss can understand. Although I can't know *exactly* how they feel, this shared experience forges an empathetic connection. As I sat with a bereaved parent of only a few days, she confessed, "When Miles died, I knew you were hurting, but I didn't understand or couldn't imagine how deep and devastating your pain was, until now. This is a pain only another parent who's lost a child can understand or feel."

After Miles's transition, I learned more about empathy at a deeper level. My loss had created a bond with other parents who also shared the child loss experience, which requires few words be spoken. As a bereaved parent, I understand what it means to witness and feel sadness and sorrow for another parent's loss. I hurt with them, connect with them, sharing many feelings and thoughts, and understand their tears and laments. The agony and despair of other grieving parents compels me to offer comfort and a safe place of refuge. I respect and support their efforts to make it through each minute, hour, and day, because I know my own struggles. It's in those quiet moments that the power of empathy allows us to be the most human, especially when we don't know what to say.

When You Don't Know What to Say

Most of us have encountered situations when we don't know exactly what to say to the bereaved. Silence is uncomfortable, and we want to fill the void. Usually when we say, "I'm sorry for your loss," "I'm sorry for your pain," or "You have my condolences," we've said enough.

When we show empathy and are present, sitting silently with the grieving person, they sense our comfort. At a time when words fail, our listening and sympathetic ear can be more consolatory than searching for the right words. Our presence speaks comfort, validates a person's pain, and communicates that we're there for them. They're not alone in their grief.

However, the intentionality of our presence is often misguided when we turn the focus away from the griever and place it on ourselves. This is not the best time to share unsolicited accounts of your own grief experience, which minimizes the griever's personal loss. One such instance was shared by a friend who had recently lost her father, and an acquaintance called to extend condolences.

"I wish I hadn't answered the phone," Jenny said. "The conversation began okay, but after a few minutes, she began telling me about a death *she* had experienced years ago. Before long, I was consoling her. She forgot that my father had just passed and that I was the one grieving. By the time I got off the phone I was drained."

In other instances, inconsiderate actions, conduct, manners, and responses become problematic and lead to intense emotions for those experiencing loss. A grieving couple shared about insensitive behavior they experienced after their daughter passed. They shared their anger at how family members overstepped boundaries by asking too many probing questions and making unsolicited suggestions.

"Why can't I be part of the memorial service?"

"Shouldn't you find out why and how she died?"

"What are you going to do with her things?"

It's clear that these types of opinions aren't supportive when they cause distress and anger for the grieving person. Sympathetic and empathetic support requires humility and respect by considering our words and our behavior for the grieving person's wishes. While we can't know exactly how a grieving person feels, especially if we have not experienced the loss and grief they are experiencing, we can, however, seek to respond to loss with gentle intention.

Gentle intention asks us to put the other person first and to care about them and their present needs. When we care enough to step outside ourselves, our world, and our judgment and sit inside another person's grief and suffering, we become change agents. To be properly compassionate, sympathetic, and empathetic in grief demands continuous growth and vulnerability in each of us. When we become students and teachers in grief, we progress into a society that no longer feels inadequate when addressing and responding to mourning. We honor the grief and the person who is grieving.

Moving Forward

At its core compassion is being present, sitting silently with the grieving person, which often brings deepest comfort at a time when words fail us. Our listening and genuine sympathetic ear can be more consolatory than searching for the right words. Our presence speaks ultimate support, validates the agonizing pain, and communicates fully that we're there. The grieving person knows they are not alone.

CHAPTER 4

Reexamining What to Say to Grieving People

*I see people, as they approach me, trying to make up
their minds whether they'll "say something about
it" or not. I hate if they do, and if they don't.*

—C. S. Lewis

WHILE THERE ARE NO magic words or expressions that will provide comfort to those who are grieving, there are certain words and expressions that can be avoided. This chapter provides a list of common expressions that may be painful or damaging to a grieving person, and offers an explanation of why.

In 1961, psychiatrist Robert Jay Lifton popularized the term cliché in his book *Thought Reform and the Psychology of Totalism: A Study of Brainwashing.* A summary of Lifton's view on clichés are thought-terminating phrases that condense the most complicated human difficulties into short, easily memorized and expressed definitive-sounding phrases, which some are conditioned to habitually repeat to themselves and to other people. This concept holds true today because such phrases tend to minimize the complexity of grief.

In my experience and that of countless bereaved people with whom I've spoken, the common grief experience we've encountered occurred when other people inflicted deep emotional and spiritual distress through clichés and platitudes. These words left us feeling angry, offended, and that our grief had been minimized.

Avoid Clichés

After a loved one dies, well-meaning family and friends show love, comfort, and support by sharing words of condolence meant to lift the bereaved person's spirits. Though filled with good intentions, these clichés often leave hurting people burdened with anger and guilt. They're grateful to have support but dread the unintended pain those statements cause.

Although those expressions are generally accepted as kind responses and inquiries, it's often difficult for the griever to reveal their dissent because their grief exists in the layers of their lives. We don't want to offend anyone, but we're wounded by the significant impact they have on those who mourn.

Most people comfortably repeat clichés. These words avoid true emotions and are generally automatic responses. Usually empty phrases tend to cover up their feelings and keep things superficial, which has little personal involvement. And while some of these clichés may be true, they aren't comforting to the grieving person.

When we're willing to examine and eliminate phrases that don't serve the well-being of the bereaved, we cause change and growth in ourselves and in our sphere of influence that enlighten and educate us and others toward extending sympathy. When we offer sympathy, we exchange our common clichés and platitudes and become empowered to speak kind, gentle, loving words that reveal our true intention in extending sympathy. In chapters 2 and 3, I've referred to some of those well-used, meaningless phrases. Now let's look at why they don't help and learn about ideas for what we can say or do instead.

Common Clichés and Platitudes that Cause Pain

1. "Time heals all wounds." Time *alone* doesn't heal wounds. Healing requires work and is influenced by what grievers do with their time to help facilitate healing.

Instead, consider saying something like: "You're hurting badly. The pain never fully goes away, but over time, it will become easier to carry."

2. "They're in a better place." While many believe this is true, it's not comforting to someone mourning the death of a family member or friend. When heartbroken and engulfed in grief's intense pain, there's no *better place* the bereaved person wants their loved one to be than physically there with them.

Instead, pause, listen, and ask how the bereaved feels. Refer to their loneliness and pain. Focus on the hurting person, not the deceased.

3. "You've been like this long enough." "It's time to get on with your life." "Move on." "Just get over it." The unspoken meaning of these statements imply the speaker is impatient or uncomfortable with someone's grieving process.

Each person grieves at their own pace and in their own way because their relationship with the person they lost is different from anyone else's. We don't get over someone and simply move on; we learn to carry and integrate their absence into our daily lives as we learn to move forward. Grief changes with time—and may never end, because grief takes as long as it takes.

Instead, try something like this: "You're still in great pain, and I'm sorry. I know it may take a long time before you feel better. Do you feel like talking about it?"

4. "You have your entire life ahead of you." Losing someone we love can be overwhelming, and grievers often can't imagine making it through each day. Pushing them to envision a future life without their loved one only adds intensity and insult to their pain.

Instead, another option might be: "You've gone through a devastating loss, and in the coming months it'll be hard living with this pain. I'll be here for you."

5. "Let me know if you need anything/if I can do anything for you." Mourning is exhausting and mentally draining. When experiencing shock and pain, those who grieve often don't have the energy or focus to identify their immediate needs. Because the loss of their loved one consumes them, most grievers won't ask for help.

Instead, extend compassion and offer to provide specific help—run errands, cook a meal, assist with the children, and clean.

6. "I know just how you feel." Everyone experiences grief differently, and it's impossible to know *exactly* how an individual feels in their unique situation. Though someone may have experienced a similar loss, when a person's grieving, it's probably not the appropriate time to talk about that unless the griever asks.

Instead, keep the focus on the griever and their loss. If you've experienced a similar loss, you can provide valuable support, but refrain from suggesting you know *exactly* what they're going through.

7. "Everything happens for a reason." When loss happens, how do you know there's a reason? Even if you might know the reason, it changes nothing. Grievers still hurt. Some deaths seem senseless and out of order.

Instead, don't attempt to offer a reason or rationale. Be available to listen. Say something like, "I can't imagine how you're feeling right now."

8. "It happened for the best." These words sound cold and harsh, and are painful for mourners to hear. Whose best did someone's death happen for? No one wants to hear that having their loved one die was the best outcome.

Avoid these type of statements and refrain from assuming you have answers to why the deceased died. Instead, remain sensitive to the feelings of those mourning.

9. "Don't cry." "Don't cry, it might upset your mother/father/sister/brother." "He/she wouldn't want you to cry or be sad." Sadness and crying are natural responses to the death of someone we love. Suppressing your feelings won't allow people to grieve fully. Such statements create guilt and place a burden on grievers that their sadness or tears will cause someone else's pain. Embracing sadness by crying is a healthy way of handling the death of someone we love.

Instead, be willing to sit with them and witness their agony and tears of grief without judgment or a need to make yourself feel more comfortable around grieving people. Avoid statements that tell a grieving person how to feel. Offering hugs and a shoulder to lean on, as well as the following expressions can be helpful: "It's okay to weep and feel your grief. You don't have to apologize for your sadness or tears, it's expected in a loss such as yours."

10. "Be strong/stay strong." This statement takes away permission to grieve. Grieving people shouldn't feel obligated to be strong or deny the pain of losing someone.

There are times when they'll temporarily suppress pain until they're in a safe place to release it. But they need to allow themselves to feel and express their emotions and work through their grief. Being strong doesn't mean we don't allow ourselves to experience the full emotions of grief, nor does it mean we're weak when we do.

Instead, consider: "Take time to grieve in your own way. Don't feel you have to suppress your pain and appear strong. I can't imagine how hard this must be for you."

11. "What doesn't kill you makes you stronger." "This will make you stronger." For some, it can also shatter their lives into pieces, make them weaker, and in some cases, may even lead to death.

Mourners grieve in the present and can't think about what their future will be like. Such statements pull them away from their present pain. It's often unimaginable for the bereaved to see themselves stronger in the future as the result of their loss.

Eliminate this statement when talking to mourners. Consider this response instead: "I can't imagine the pain you're feeling. You're doing the best you can in this situation, don't give up."

12. "It was God's will." "It was their time." During a time when grievers often struggle with the spiritual questions about their loved one's transition, these statements imply that there's a rational explanation for their loss. Hearing this doesn't usually help because it implies

your discomfort with the situation and further shifts them away from their pain.

Instead, try: "Nothing I can say is going to stop the hurt, but if you want to talk about it, I'm here to listen."

13. "Stay busy; don't think about it." Avoiding or suppressing thoughts and feelings of grief can be harmful if done continuously or over an extended period.

Consider saying this instead: "Take time to care for yourself and tend to your emotional, physical, and spiritual needs."

14. "They did what they came here to do." This may be true, but not in all instances. For those whose loved one transitioned at a young age, or whom they believe didn't get to live a full life, their death will always be too soon. Those who grieve need to process their grief and arrive at that determination on their own, in order to accept that concept.

Instead, try: "They did a lot of good, touched a lot of lives, and will be missed greatly."

15. "God has another angel/needed another angel." This empty statement doesn't provide comfort. It's often said that many people are comfortable making such statements—as long as it isn't their child that God needed as an angel. Our loved one didn't die because God needed another angel.

Think about saying this instead: "I can't imagine the pain you're feeling and I'm so sorry. I know you miss them greatly." This keeps the focus on them and their pain.

16. "God doesn't make any mistakes." Often the grieving person's world is shattered and feels things are out of order and terribly wrong.

In some situations, such as in the death of a child, such a statement comes across as harsh and that God caused the death. Even for some who hold religious beliefs, it often takes time and work to understand God's presence in their loss.

Instead, perhaps consider saying this: "Losing a loved one is painful and I'm sorry you're hurting so badly."

17. "God doesn't give you more than you can handle." This implies that the bereaved shouldn't feel the intensity of grief because God placed it on them. Some people can't handle the death of someone they love. Mourners frequently feel that the overwhelming pain of grief is more than they can handle and that they'll never move beyond their agony.

Instead, try to be present and supportive while acknowledging their pain.

18. "You're the man/woman of the house now." Saying this to a child/teen dealing with grief places an enormous burden on them to take on the responsibility of secondary losses and can lead to guilt and resentment.

Instead, say this: "I know you'll miss your mom/dad/loved one deeply. I'm here to help in any way I can."

19. "If I were you, I would . . ." Offering unsolicited advice is disrespectful because what works for one person might not work for someone else.

From personal experience, I suggest we only offer advice when asked. If you've had a similar experience and believe you have valuable insight, and some advice might be helpful and even comforting, such as, "I've also lost a child, and I sense the pain . . .," or "I'm available to share my experience, and what I learned/what helped me, if you'd like," may help. These statements focus on the griever.

20. "Try to look for the good in the situation. Be positive; something good will come of this." Most grievers would trade any future good that might come rather than have their loved one die. Though good may eventually prevail, it's not a trade-off for the death of a loved one. And again, it moves the focus away from their pain.

It's best not to try and fix the situation or find good in it. Instead, show support by acknowledging their loss and pain: "I can see how deeply hurtful this is and I'm here whenever you need me."

21. "There are people worse off than you." Comparing someone else's loss to the griever's situation minimizes their pain and invalidates their mourning.

Avoid comparison and instead, validate the mourner's loss by showing compassion and sympathy for their situation.

22. "At least" statements. At least statements imply mourners shouldn't be sad, but grateful because they had/have the experience that follows the "At least" statement. For example,

"At least you have/can have other children." Children aren't replaceable.

"At least you're young, you can remarry." People aren't replaceable.

"At least they didn't suffer," or "At least she/he is out of pain." The griever's pain remains.

While the phrases "At least you had them for as long as you did," or "At least they lived a good/long life" may be true, the mourners probably feel that they wanted their loved one around longer.

Instead, try to avoid "At least" statements. In some cases, mourners may be grateful for the noted experience; however, it doesn't take away their pain of missing the deceased.

These suggestions provide a guideline for initiating meaningful thought and discussion among grievers, sympathizers, and other supportive communities to help build a communication process that eliminates those offensive actions and promotes a kinder, more informed exchange. Each of us is responsible for choosing compassionate, sincere, and thoughtful words that reflect our individual situation when extending heartfelt expressions of genuine sympathy. When we're intentional about the language we use, we invite other grievers, their supporters, and the larger community to join us and begin practicing those guidelines, forming a grief community to grow and heal together.

Moving Forward

When we're willing to examine and eliminate insensitive phrases that imply a disservice to the well-being of the bereaved, we cause change. We invite others to join us on a genuine journey of growing and learning to express empathy and compassion that supports the bereaved. Change happens in our hearts, minds, and spirits when we become aware of the impact of our words and determine to make a difference. Asking ourselves, "How might I feel if someone said that to me?" and considering alternative expressions that convey a deeper care and concern help to connect with others on a more empathetic and compassionate level. We become empowered to exchange offensive words for effective dialogue that reveals our true intention in extending sympathy.

_____
_____
_____
_____
_____
_____
_____
_____
_____
_____
_____
_____
_____
_____
_____
_____
_____
_____
_____
_____
_____
_____
_____
_____
_____
_____
_____
_____
_____
_____
_____
_____
_____
_____
_____

CHAPTER 5

When Our Faith Is Shaken

*Fear not, for I am with you; be not dismayed, for
I am your God; I will strengthen you, I will help you,
I will uphold you with my righteous right hand.*

Isaiah 41:10

Blessed are those who mourn, for they will be comforted.

—Jesus, Matthew 5:4

WHEN A LOVED ONE dies, we often have many unanswered questions. Depending on the circumstances of their transition, some might say God's not fair or he's punishing grievers for some misdeed.

After Miles died, a spiritual tornado shook through the foundation on which I live my life—my faith. I'd grown up in the church and, as an adult, remained actively involved, serving in a leadership role at my local place of worship. I couldn't understand how this devastating storm had left my world in ruin. My faith was shaken. I had questions and cried out for answers.

God, Why?

Growing up I often heard people say, "You shouldn't question God," which didn't feel right to me, even then, because I had questions I believed only he could answer. As I grew older, I learned I could talk to him and present my questions, concerns, and anything else on my mind without fear that he'd become vengeful or punish me.

On many days after Miles's death, it seemed God was silent. I couldn't hear his voice or feel his presence. I couldn't understand how that terrible thing could've happened to my child. I had questions. "God, where were you?" I lamented. "Why did you allow my child to die?" I cried out for answers—something, anything that would make sense out of a loss that seemed unbearable.

During those times, I felt alone and abandoned, yet my faith told me otherwise. Despite my lack of feeling, I knew he was with me, carrying me through each agonizing day.

Still, my faith was shaken and I questioned the certainty of my spiritual beliefs. From the early hours after Miles transitioned, I knew I'd have to lean against my religious foundation to survive such devastating loss. My church family remained beside me with an outpouring of encouragement, love, and support.

Donna, a beloved woman at our church, had adopted our family when we first moved to Colorado. My husband, Bob, and I were her son and daughter and the boys her grandchildren. During the years following Miles's death, when I needed encouragement, Donna would remind me of the night Miles passed. Entering the waiting room, I found it packed with our friends and church family.

"You went to every person in there and held their hands in yours," she said. "You looked into their eyes and said, 'We've got to trust God.'"

"We've got to trust God" became a principle that I anguished over *and* relied on to carry me through my intense sorrow.

"I don't agree with what happened to my child. If you'd asked me, I would've said no. But I still trust you," I said to God as I bemoaned my loss. From the moment we found Miles in his room, unresponsive, our phone calls had initiated a prayer chain at our church, and family and friends across the nation were praying for him. I'd prayed for my son to live, and so had others.

When I was pacing back and forth on the street in front of my home as the paramedic administered aid to my sweet Miles, I had prayed, "God, please let him live. He will live and not die. He will live and not die. He will live and not die." I believed with all the assurance inside me that his life would be spared.

But God had said no and let me down.

I felt crushed. "Why weren't my prayers enough to save my child? Why did others live, but Miles died?"

Over the years, my husband and sons and I had prayed for others, family and friends we knew personally and others in the body of Christ, and they had lived. Miles had joined in many of those prayers, and yet when he became the one others were interceding for, he had died.

Did God have favorites?

Faith Doesn't Exempt Us from Grieving

Many people in the religious community teach that if we have enough faith, God will grant whatever we pray for. If we want a new car and have enough faith, then we'll get it. If we're sick, we'll receive divine healing, or if we pray for a loved one to live, they won't die. And perhaps some people feel spiritually inferior or guilty when they pray for someone to live, and that person dies.

"You shouldn't be sad. He's in heaven with God," some might say.

When we endure immense heartbreak and distress, our hearts and our heads seem to send opposing messages. It's hard to reconcile what we know in our heart with what we think and feel.

Shouldn't I be happy he's with God or isn't suffering anymore?

We pray for the pain to go away, but it remains.

I'd understood that although faith is the bedrock that determines how I live my life, it doesn't always overrule, cancel, or change the outcome of things I experience. I felt my prayers on Miles's behalf still hadn't been enough. And I became angry because I felt that God had hurt me.

God Can Handle Our Anger

Jan and I attended the same church in Colorado years earlier. A friend texted and asked if I could meet with Jan because she was struggling with her son's death. Miles had died a year after Jan's son. We sat in a corner booth at a small neighborhood restaurant and had barely begun our conversation when Jan interrupted me. "Gwen." The inflection of her voice alerted me that something intense would follow.

Two years had passed, and her raw heartbreak and fragile faith spewed from the words she spoke. "Let me say right now, I don't want to hear anything about God. God took my only child from me. Why did God let my son die?" Her voice was soft but firm. Tears puddled at the corners of her eyes as she lowered her voice to barely a whisper. She wrapped her hands around the glass of water in front of her. "I miss him so much and I don't know how I can make it without him. God knew James was all I had."

Her statements didn't shock me. Anger is a stage of grief that many grievers experience. I empathized with her pain. Just as the reality of loss sets in, so can anger. It's a natural response to a perceived wrong. Deep disappointment, hard-hearted feelings, and offense are common emotions that can surface when, for example, we feel that our loved one was snatched from us, or that we've been betrayed, or treated unfairly. Anger can be directed at ourselves, other people, our deceased loved one, society, or at God.

"I was angry at God," George, a devout Christian friend, shared with me over the phone. When Miles first died, he had shared part of his story with Bob and I to encourage us. George said he would share more later.

Now I asked him to share more of his grief experience with me. I could hear the passion in his voice as I pressed the phone to my ear. "I'd trusted God to deliver my son and believed he would bring him home, like he had the prodigal son. I'd stood faithfully, prayed Scripture over his life, and never imagined I'd wake up one morning to learn my child had died. I felt God had let me down."

I understood George's anger and disappointment. There was a time when I also questioned if the promises of Scripture really applied to me, and I was angry.

God, is your Word true? had echoed through my mind for years.

A lot of us are taught that being mad at God for allowing the death of a loved one dishonors him or implies we lack spiritual maturity, but it's neither. God understands our deepest despair and petitions. He's big enough and great enough to handle our anger when we are deep in grief.

Though it isn't wrong to experience roiling feelings of anger, we need to acknowledge and resolve them. When we don't have the freedom to acknowledge *all* the emotions we encounter in grief, we can go through life carrying unresolved feelings that leave us spiritually stagnant and unable to move forward and toward healing. When we allow these emotions to settle in our hearts over an extended period of time, we begin to harbor dishonor and disrespect, which can cause us to abandon our relationship with God.

For example, a child or teenager angry with her parents may choose not to speak to them for a few days. Over time, her unresolved anger leads to disrespect toward her parents when she begins slamming doors, yelling, and cursing—she may even decide to leave home. That's unacceptable. Her *unresolved* anger had led her to cross a boundary that disrespected her parents, which could impact the relationship with her parents.

My own grief-based resentment wasn't an emotion that surfaced often but was hidden in avoidance, denial, and frustration.

Why hadn't I sensed something was wrong?

As a mother, I was troubled because I believed I should've known Miles was in crisis and needed me.

God, why didn't you tell me that Miles needed me?

Though Bob and I had administered CPR until the paramedics arrived, it hadn't been enough to save him.

Could I have done more?

Spiritually, I felt uncomfortable and guarded about anger in my grief. Initially, when feelings of infuriation arose, I kept them tempered and controlled, frequently pushing them inside. And when I talked about my feelings, I made sure I said the *right* things. I told myself that

I wasn't angry *at* God for allowing Miles to die, but that I felt forsaken *that* God had allowed him to die, robbing Miles of living a full life.

Yet when I looked deeper and examined my anger, I learned something that helped me to become more spiritually authentic and transparent. I'd denied and disguised and been silent about those core feelings. Truth was, I felt God had hurt me deeply, and I questioned whether he'd deserted me, ignoring the trust I placed in him.

I tried to live a good Christian life, and this happens.

Where were you when we needed you?

Miles was a wonderful son, a good person; not perfect, but he loved you, God.

I had heard no one within my close church community, family, or friends share that they'd struggled with similar faith-doubting feelings in their grief. Subconsciously, I believed I had to shield my feelings of doubt and exasperation from those around me. The weight of keeping those emotions hidden inside was more than I wanted to carry.

I wanted to be delivered from the pain and anger. I needed to confess everything I was feeling to God, and all that was hurting me, so I could be freed from my agony.

Like me, others have had similar struggles. I've found it encouraging to know that these struggles aren't a reflection of our spirituality. Many, having condemned themselves, are weighed down with guilt and judgment. I've learned that in order to move forward, I had to forgive myself when anger caused me to be too harsh with myself or with others. I had to rely on my religious convictions to work through my anger, brokenness, and confusion. Starting the faith-based GriefShare program a couple of months after Miles's transition helped me to begin releasing guilt and judgment, and to acknowledge forgiveness in grief. When I began to forgive I was able to work through and release forgiveness in a healthy way. That's when I experienced release and relief.

While we find hope and comfort in our religious beliefs, it doesn't exempt us from grieving the death of a loved one. When we struggle in grief, experiencing all those harsh emotions that might seem wrong, it doesn't imply that we're weak or inferior, nor does it mean that we aren't trusting God with our pain. When we wrestle with questions and feelings of being forsaken, I believe God honors our honesty and gives us grace and time to learn that we can trust him as we adjust to this new normal of life without our loved ones, and through this, we can experience great comfort and a closer relationship with him.

When I confessed my disappointment that he allowed my child to die, God didn't condemn me but gave me reassurance. When I asked him to give my life and my pain a greater purpose, he renewed my hope. I've gained a greater appreciation in knowing that I don't have to be strong to depend on his strength. And though I grieve, I do so with continuing faith in what I believe.

Persevering by Faith

As I continue to live with grief, I'm learning to integrate my loss with the will of God for my life. He doesn't always answer prayers in the manner we choose. We pray, and sometimes we still struggle, and bad things happen. I reminded myself repeatedly that we live in a world where bad things happen to all of us. I resolved that God wasn't busy doing something else, or made a mistake, or *caused* Miles's death. But when the circumstances of life happened, in divine wisdom, God *allowed* Miles to transition.

I may never know why God didn't allow Miles to live. But I trust him to carry me through my loss. Most days I believe that Miles completed his purpose on the earth. But on days when I struggle and hurt deeply, I remind myself to trust in God's sovereignty.

Moving Forward

Having our faith shaken and losing faith isn't the same. Shaken faith doesn't mean we are unstable. Overwhelming disappointment, loss, and pain can test our resolve and leave us bewildered. Though we may struggle, we remain committed to God. Staying committed to my ideals has taught me to persevere in my darkest times and to move forward, knowing God is always with me in all circumstances of life.

We can choose to forgive ourselves when anger causes us to be too harsh with ourselves or with others. Through forgiveness, we have the privilege of leaning on our religious convictions as we work through our anger, brokenness, and confusion. Our faith enables us to bear the difficulty of loss. We understand that God doesn't always calm the storm or lighten the pain. When we witness God's grace working in our lives, we can release the anger, condemnation, guilt, fear, and judgment as he calms and comforts, carrying us through the darkness of grief.

PART 2

Adapting to Life after Loss

CHAPTER 6

You're Not Feeling Okay

Grief is like the ocean; it comes on waves ebbing and
flowing. Sometimes the water is calm, and sometimes it
is overwhelming. All we can do is learn to swim.

—Vicki Harrison

GUTTURAL SOUNDS CRASHED THROUGH the dark recesses of my mind. I couldn't breathe. I didn't think I was going to live. The grief overpowered and consumed me. My chest felt as if it would explode from pent-up emotions and stabbing, grieving pain.

It had been almost four years since Miles's death and there were days when raw, excruciating grief still engulfed me. I sat on my deck, hoping the serenity of nature would ease the heaviness.

But nature was a blur.

Not even the flowers in bloom or the fluttering hummingbird soothed the aching.

By now most of my family and friends had moved on with their lives.

But I hadn't.

Most of my friends and family were unaware that deep grief still washed over me often, without warning, and was always present when I ached for Miles's presence. When that happened, I endured alone. Tears streamed down my face. I couldn't hold them back. I wasn't okay and needed someone to know. I couldn't trust my confession of intense sadness to just anybody. My loneliness intensified.

During these times, we doubt whether we've progressed toward healing. Fighting through tough days isn't a sign of regression or stagnation. It's possible to move forward and grow through bereavement. Growth takes place when we talk about our experiences, become vulnerable and honest about suffering, and allow ourselves the freedom to grieve.

Sharing through Times of Struggle

Like me, others living with loss experience episodes of recurrent distress. The Mayo Clinic reminds us that there's no certain point after a loved one's death that grief magically ends. Reminders will surface that bring back our pain. We hurt deeply. This doesn't mean we're stuck, dysfunctional, or aren't as strong as someone else. It's a sign that we're normal and we miss our loved ones.

Most grievers expect that there'll be days when we struggle; however, it's more challenging to tell someone when we're not okay. Admitting that we have times when grief consumes us carries a negative connotation. Confessing to others opens us up to shame and embarrassment. We dread judgment from others in regard to our inability to move forward.

We may remain quiet, suffering alone when we need support the most, instead of reaching out to someone who'll listen and provide empathy as we share our challenges.

Reality is, the longer we live with grief, the more difficult it is to acknowledge our struggles. Society tells us that talking about our sadness or loss is unacceptable. We're silenced by personal perception when we see people living freely apart from the grief we bear daily. And because we often assume they don't care, have time, or want to know about our woes, we sometimes condemn ourselves for the pain and anguish that absorbs our time and drains our energy.

Suppressing those emotions for brief periods may be necessary when addressing immediate matters, like working or taking care of the children. But ignored pain and emotional tension becomes unhealthy, and is trapped inside with no outlet for processing and releasing them.

If left unaddressed, suppressed grief over time leads to other problems: anger, depression, isolation, and even physical illness. In his book *The Body Keeps the Score*, Bessell van der Kolk says that body pain and other internal emotions can be a result of unaddressed grief. He talks about the relationship between body pain and other internal emotions, and how, when people suffer emotionally, that suffering goes beyond the mind and shows up as symptoms in their bodies. It affects things like stress, digestion, how they sit, breathe, attitudes toward exercise, and other illnesses. This further impedes our ability to move forward and grow through loss.

We hide sadness and pretend everything's fine rather than endure the backlash of grief-shaming from others. Psychotherapist, grief counselor, and author Megan Devine in the documentary *Speaking Grief* says that grief-shaming happens when people make decisions and judgments about how people mourn publicly. To some of us, it may feel less stressful to hide and suppress outward expressions of mourning than it is to share them.

We recognize we're not okay and we don't want to burden anyone with our melancholic story or aren't sure they care. Yet many grieving hearts yearn for someone safe and nonjudgmental to listen and offer reassurance. Fear stops us from pursuing the solace we need to navigate and grow through these times. We're reluctant to become vulnerable and honest about living with the death of a loved one. Confiding in someone provides comfort and support and helps us to process our loss.

I spent days suppressing the need to share my agony when anxiety kept me from reaching out for support. I yearned for relief and desired to grieve without judgment or false assumptions.

Should I be transparent when I'm not okay?

Could I take a chance and reach out to someone?

Moving forward required me to take responsibility for how I managed and coped with loss. Choosing to either grieve alone or reach out to someone was a choice only I could make.

My tears hadn't stopped, but I began to wipe them away. I pushed my chair back, walked across the deck, leaned forward on the rails, and stared at the stump of the dead tree our family had cut down, one of the last family activities we'd shared, just two weeks before Miles passed. I had a safe confidante with whom I could share those times of emotional struggle. For over twenty years we'd walked through some of life's happy and challenging experiences together—family, faith, career, and any other encounters.

My heart pounding, I dialed my friend's phone number. The cell phone rested against my cheek as I swallowed and forced the words past the dry lump stuck in my throat.

"It hurts so bad, and I miss him so much," I said to my best friend.

And that's when vulnerability started pushing back the darkness and began a genuine conversation.

Becoming Vulnerable

Allowing others to share and witness our grief demands courage and trust. We agonize over possible, unintended consequences of adding to the sadness and pain we already endure. The natural tendency to protect ourselves and ease the internal struggle sends us into defensive mode. Most of us fight the urge to shut down and isolate, even as we wrestle with the desire for someone to accompany us through our mourning. But as we lower the emotional barriers we've placed around our loss and accept the risks of revealing our brokenness, heartache, and private struggles, we begin to experience a sense of security because the person listening with empathy or compassion makes us feel safe.

In the past, appearing vulnerable frightened me. Memories of past rejection, misunderstandings, and betrayals filled my mind. My grief was mine alone and I didn't want to risk opening myself to someone who wouldn't understand what I was going through. I couldn't allow their unreasonable expectations to dictate how I should feel, what I should do, or how I should grieve. Now, engulfed in the agony of grief, I wrestled with questions.

Is it safe to tell anyone, "I'm not okay"?

What if I open myself to someone and they minimize my pain?

What if I embarrass myself?

I hesitated to appear needy or whiny. For many of us, transparency can be frightening because it challenges us to risk judgment or abandonment. Our desire for comfort and support conflicts with our doubt, anxiety, and the fear that our worst "what ifs" might become reality.

For me, becoming vulnerable was a stressful process. Early betrayals and emotional injury had broken my trust and I became skilled at suppressing emotions and did so for much of my life. I believed vulnerability was a weakness, or at its best, a breach of my protective armor.

In *Daring Greatly*, Brené Brown conveys that being vulnerable doesn't mean we are weak, but rather, being vulnerable means we must decide whether we will courageously engage with our vulnerability. To willingly own and engage with the uncertainty, risk, and emotional exposure we confront every day determines how well we understand our purpose.

Up until now, I had fought against opening up and allowing others into the most painful areas of my life. Reaching out and displaying courage in these instances made me apprehensive.

But I did it.

I believed there were those with whom I could be transparent. To trust someone with our grief, we must feel safe with them. Trust allows us to connect with those willing to sit with us, listen to us, cry with us, and just *be* with us. But while I was in the throes of despair, the struggle to reach out and admit I was hurting magnified, demanding greater courage. Courage is often viewed as a display of tenacious boldness or bravery, and while this can be true, courage is also revealed in quiet and seemingly unheroic ways.

My most courageous acts manifest in simple-but-valiant ways, embodied when I pick up the phone, call a trusted friend, and say, "I'm having a hard day."

Freedom to Grieve Unapologetically

On my lowest and most painful days, I've found strength and freedom by affirming my struggles. I began to honor my journey when

I began to grieve authentically rather than apologetically. Being truthful about the reality of my loss led to growth. I've learned to reject feelings of guilt or embarrassment when grief pangs overwhelm me and I'm hurting deeply.

Many people never experience the freedom to grieve fully and remain captive to reactions, opinions, and misconceptions rather than tending to their own emotional needs. Overcoming the pressure to conform to expectations of others enables us to acknowledge and work through the myriad emotions that bombard us. When we allow ourselves to fully grieve, we're free to be honest, feel, express, and talk about our loss. We can learn to be present with sadness, anger, emptiness, and other emotions that surface.

Through my grief journey, I've grown to respect my pain, and not to hide, suppress, or isolate myself in it. I become empowered when I embrace a truth—that my grieving process will take as long as it takes. I've learned not to apologize for my tears, to accept there'll be days when I'm not okay, and to reach out to trusted loved ones for support when I need it.

Moving Forward

When trust exists, we're able to be transparent about our anguish and relieve the pressure to conform to *acceptable* ways to grieve. It allows those living with grief to break out of self-limiting boundaries surrounding loss. As transparency from shame transforms into vulnerable sharing, we become stronger and empowered. Strength is cloaked in the freedom to grieve in our own sacred way, empowering us to admit when our heartache is tender and we're not feeling okay. To trust someone with our grief, we must feel safe with them. Trust allows us to connect with those willing to sit with us, listen to us, cry with us, and just *be* with us.

CHAPTER 7

"Just Get Over It"

The reality is that you will grieve forever. You will not "get over" the loss of a loved one; you will learn to live with it. You will heal, and you will rebuild yourself around the loss you have suffered. You will be whole again, but you will never be the same. Nor should you be the same, nor would you want to.

—Elisabeth Kübler-Ross and David Kessler

"JUST GET OVER IT," they say.

"It's time to get on with your life."

"You've been like this long enough."

"Stop feeling sorry for yourself and move on."

Moving through grief sometimes takes longer than the bereaved expect, or how long society accommodates. As time passes, people who are supporting those grieving may become impatient and uncomfortable.

Can't Rush Grief

The persistence of others to rush the bereaved through the mourning process often arises from a desire *for their own comfort*. For them, sadness and heartache cloud the atmosphere. Family and friends become frustrated with what they regard as our lack of progress toward returning to the person we were before our loss.

What often begins as compassion for someone's loss turns to comparison, then judgment. Over time, if the bereaved person is hesitant to laugh, socialize, start new relationships, or clear out belongings, those who are supporting them might imply the bereaved are *wallowing* in grief.

The push toward normalcy extends beyond our immediate circle. It's deeply rooted within society, and we're taught to comply with artificial timelines and criteria. The length of our sorrow is connected to the relationship with the person we lost. Grieving a child, parent, spouse, partner, sibling, grandparent, or other family member carries a projection of how long mourning should take.

Regardless of the family connection, those schedules are inadequate. For instance, after death happens to a close person in our lives, we're typically granted three to five days bereavement leave from our jobs. Generous employers may grant a few more. Grieving people are enduring the most shattering, heartbreaking event of their lives, and their thoughts and emotions are a tangled web of raw pain, shock, and daze.

Yet most employers assume employees can return to work and function at a fairly normal capacity, but those unreasonable demands minimize death's magnitude and pressure us to place another's desire for comfort above our need to mourn fully. Some family, friends, and others may have good intentions and want hurting people to move past their pain to a happier life. However, the results of their actions are the same as when we suggest that mourners dismiss their pain and get on with living.

Before Miles transitioned, I sought to help those who grieved move forward when I said that the deceased "wouldn't want you to be sad." Yes, I was one of those people who had offered assumptions. But I soon learned that when we claim to know what a deceased person would say or want, we make assumptions that project guilt and confusion, which does little, if anything, to help the bereaved move forward. We can't truly know what someone would want unless that information has been shared with us.

When we tell someone it's time to *get over* a loved one's death or time to *move on,* it communicates an unspoken message. We infer that something or someone else can replace the relationship or the place held by our loss, and our continued heartache is unwarranted.

We don't *get over* a loved one's death, we learn to live with a loved one's death, which provides understanding that enables us to give and receive compassionate support outside the dictates of timelines.

I Can't Just *Move On*

"It's been six months, a year, or longer since your loved one died. It's time to move on." Some who have never experienced the death of a close loved one, or may not understand the complexity of the stages of grief and the time it takes to move through the grief process may believe that mourning follows defined stages and timelines. No one adheres to defined stages or strict timelines, cultural norms, or projected expectations nor can they *just move on*. We should give grace and empathy for each person's individual process, for them to grieve differently, in their own time and in their own way. None of us experiences grief the same, so we shouldn't project our expectations onto anyone else.

For example, after Miles transitioned, it took me five-and-a-half years to pack up the belongings in his bedroom. That doesn't mean that I should project my timeline or emotional process onto other grieving parents. For some people it may take less or more time. Each person and their unique circumstances determine what and when the time is right for them. Not anyone else.

Meeting a grieving person where they are and supporting them in the way that they need us is like a gift to them. Transformation takes place when empathy with *words* steps backs and bows graciously as empathy with *action* walks beside the grieving person at a time when gentle actions and understanding of the lasting impact of loss are what's needed.

"I was going through the motions of living but my family, friends, and church members, thought I was doing good," my friend and business associate, George, recounted during our phone conversation.

"I wasn't. My son's death left me traumatized. You don't just get over it or move on from something like that."

Eleven-and-a-half months after Miles's death, I was standing at my kitchen sink, washing dishes when my eyes rested on a red memorial wristband we'd given out at his Celebration of Life service. A deep stabbing ache sat in my chest. I couldn't breathe and began to pant heavily. Feelings of overwhelming agony washed over me and I squeezed my eyes shut attempting to stop the flowing tears.

He's not away at college.

He's not living in another state or serving in the military in a foreign country.

My child died.

While many presumed I'd progressed beyond days of intense pain, I was only beginning to accept my son's death. Over the past year, I'd stared hollow-eyed at the wristband hanging on the candelabra on the countertop many times, but in *this* moment, I realized that Miles wasn't coming home.

The second year after my loss, my anguish remained deep and intense. Though the initial shock had lifted, I'd suffered through the *first* milestones and events. That's when the magnitude of living every day without Miles became more distressful.

Acceptance of our loss comes in each person's own time. Until then it's helpful for those supporting grieving people to understand that talking with us, walking beside us, sitting with us can help us not to feel alone and abandoned when we need to be supported the most.

Don't Avoid Us

Sometimes those whom we thought we could depend on for support avoid contact with us. They see us, refuse to meet our eye, rush in another direction, or divert their attention to something or someone else.

Katherine and I had recently met through a mutual friend and were rooming together at a conference. We were settling in for the evening and began to talk about our loved ones who had transitioned. Katherine explained,

> My mother and brother passed within eight weeks of each other. I was devastated, in shock, hurting badly, and trying to wrap my mind around what had happened. Furthermore, I was responsible for managing their estates and providing support to other family members.
>
> What surprised and hurt me at the same time was that some people, even family, withdrew and distanced themselves. It seemed as if they thought I carried some type of bad luck or contagious death vibe that I would pass along to them.
>
> And more painful and what disappointed me the most was the change in my relationship with some of my Christian brothers and sisters. It broke my heart even more when they distanced themselves from me, as if to imply that God was punishing me for some evil deed or sin I'd committed. I never knew that someone's death could make people behave like that. I never knew people would avoid me and I'd lose friends.

I'd met Linda through another grieving mother. We sat at my dining room table, chatting and looking at support resources on my laptop computer. Linda shared, "It angers me when people won't come around me or act as if the death of my child is a contagious disease or plague that will transfer to them."

These actions are often unconscious and stem from an unfounded fear that something might happen to someone they love. While they may be unaware, it can still be hurtful to the bereaved.

In other instances, some people avoid saying our deceased's name or acknowledging their passing during conversations. "I don't want to upset him," or "I don't want her to cry," people might say. These actions generally leave the bereaved feeling their loss was disregarded or dismissed.

"We think about our loved ones every day, and sometimes we cry every day," Vickie said while we sat in the wingback chairs in the hotel lobby, waiting to be seated in the restaurant for lunch. "When someone says their name or shares a story about them, it doesn't upset me. It reminds me they haven't forgotten my husband."

Sometimes it can be difficult to know what the bereaved prefers, but it's usually safe to follow their lead. When unsure, I typically convey that I want to respect their wishes and ask whether it's okay to talk or share a story about their loved one.

I'm fortunate to have abundant support from family and friends, but it hurt me when one friend I thought would support me didn't call me or even acknowledge Miles's transition. Over the years, I'd supported and encouraged her during several difficult situations she had encountered.

Three years after Miles's transition, I saw her. I walked up to her after a meeting we had both attended. I smiled. "Hey there, how are you?" I asked.

"Hey, Gwen, I'm good." Though her words greeted me, her face did not.

We stood in the lobby outside the conference room as other people buzzed around us. The air between us was uncomfortable and strained. But we were happy to see one another.

"Miles passed away," I said, hopeful she would offer an explanation, maybe an apology, or even hug me.

"I know."

She offered no other acknowledgment and was notably uneasy.

I smiled and moved to another topic.

Though it pained me that she was unavailable to offer support, I've grown to understand and realize that others may not have the ability or emotional capacity to support those who grieve. I have learned to extend grace to them and respect their commitment to care for their own needs. When both those who grieve and those whom we look to for support seek to understand the other person and do not judge, we can maintain relationships that might otherwise become broken.

We don't know exactly why others pull away or avoid grieving people—there can be many reasons. Perhaps they don't know how to support grieving people. Maybe they are having a hard time working through their own feelings. You might find yourself in a similar situation where you've pulled away from a family member or friend who's grieving. It's okay to acknowledge and talk about your feelings.

Grief Can't Be *Fixed*

Watching someone suffering the difficulty of loss is hard, and many feel compelled to help those who hurt reach an ideal outcome. Society, movies, and books promote a fairytale narrative that, despite the most difficult and grueling experiences, we should pursue and obtain a happy and heroic ending. That portrayal reinforces the belief that those who grieve over an extended period are broken. Someone must intervene and *fix* their grief.

Eleanor Haley from the *What's Your Grief* podcast says that people want us to stop feeling pain, but grief is normal, not dysfunctional. As long as the loss was someone significant to us, grief will exist. The intensity will change over time but we recover from that loss. We won't ever return to *normal*.

Once we discover an unconscious bias or impatience toward a person's grieving process, we're responsible for resisting the urge to rush in to remedy their situation. We learn that grieving people aren't broken and don't need to be fixed. We're *heartbroken*, and the effects impact every area of our lives—often for an extended period of time.

Love doesn't stop when someone dies. When death ravages our world, we can't replace or recover what we've lost, and we can't get over the life we shared with our beloved. The precious memories remain with us forever.

Moving through Grief

During the eighteen-hour drive when our family moved from Alabama to Colorado, our then three- and six-year-old sons repeatedly asked, "Are we there yet? How long before we get there?"

Unlike road trips, mourning doesn't have a final destination or predetermined roadmap. There's no timeline we can identify with certainty. Similar to the inquiring and impatient child, some people want to know if we've arrived at the place where they're comfortable sharing space with us again.

Moving through grief may not lead to a place where we'll never feel the impact of loss. As much as we love heroic endings, in the death of someone we love, happily ever after doesn't exist. Each of us determines what an acceptable outcome looks like as we learn to live with loss. Bereavement isn't a condition that we *recover* from. It's a natural process that enables each person to carry, adjust, readjust, and carve out a path to move forward at their own pace.

When we show compassion, patience, respect, and sensitivity for each person's unique grieving process, we learn to accept that moving through grief takes as long as it takes, even if it lasts a lifetime.

Moving Forward

When someone we loved dies, we can't just get over it. Showing support beyond perceived timelines or expectations helps the griever feel supported and enables them to move forward toward healing. Your empathetic support becomes a gift.

CHAPTER 8

Holidays, Milestones, the Unexpected, and Secondary Losses

At the rising sun and at its going down; We remember them.
At the blowing of the wind and in the chill of winter; We remember them.
At the opening of the buds and in the rebirth of spring; We remember them.
At the blueness of the skies and in the warmth of summer; We remember them.
At the rustling of the leaves and in the beauty of the autumn; We remember them.
At the beginning of the year and when it ends; We remember them.
As long as we live, they too will live, for they are now a part of us as we remember them.

—Excerpt from *A Litany of Remembrance* by
Sylvan Karmens and Rabbi Jack Reimer

"DON'T WORRY ABOUT THIS old man. I'm just missing my mom, especially this time of year."

When I read Johnny's social media post, I understood his anguish. His mother had passed fifteen years earlier, and he'd stated that the holidays, her birthday, and Mother's Day are still frequently difficult for him.

I understood his feelings, and others responded, acknowledging that the passing years don't erase the sadness of missing loved ones on special occasions.

Certain Difficult Days

Living with grief is exhausting and drains our emotions, minds, and bodies. Navigating special events like holidays, birthdays, and other milestones is often brutal—even years after someone dies. And, for the newly bereaved, these occasions can be daunting.

I recall little about the first two years after Miles's transition. A thick mental fog and intense emotional despair engulfed me. When I faced days that held significant memories, I feared my inability to withstand the overwhelming agony of his death.

How will I survive this day or season without Miles being here?
How can I celebrate or be happy again?

I longed to sleep through those times that were normally fraught with loneliness, sadness, and guilt.

"I called you on that first Thanksgiving and you were so sad," my brother recounted. "I told myself I didn't want you to spend Christmas alone, so we flew to Colorado to be with you."

Until that conversation three-and-a-half years later, I hadn't remembered that my brother and his family spent Christmas with us. That memory hid behind the dark cloud in which I'd existed.

What I *do* recall is the dread that weighed on me and the anxiety that plagued me with each impending holiday season and memorable event. I felt tormented when I thought of life continuing, joy and laughter filling the atmosphere, and Miles not being there to enjoy it.

I avoided festivities and yearned to escape the agony of life without my son. Bob and I declined invitations to join friends for Thanksgiving dinner. When I saw Christmas decorations or heard seasonal music, I ached inside, which intensified the agony of missing my son.

Grief replaced the happiness and anticipation of celebrations with deep mourning, and I soon learned that this panoply of emotions wasn't confined to only holidays.

Anxiety about Significant Events

Most of us who've experienced the death of a loved one can relate to the anxiety that precedes a memorable date or event. We expect that certain days may be tearful and usually sense the assault on our emotions. We become nervous, stressed, anxious, short-tempered, and even depressed.

I struggled through the misery of the first Thanksgiving and Christmas after Miles passed. But on New Year's Eve, all the heartache I carried erupted and overshadowed me. I had no desire to do anything or go anywhere. For the first year that I could remember, I didn't go to church to celebrate the annual watchnight service—a religious celebration rooted in cultural history I'd attended since childhood.

Instead, I lay curled up in bed all day. Depressed. Filled with despair. And wept.

How can I enter a new year without my child?

Am I abandoning Miles by entering a new year without him?

Sometimes the flood of emotions doesn't set in until after an expected day has come and gone. Then, the fear and anxiety are worse than the days we're dreading.

I feared the first year commemoration of Miles's transition. For a month leading up to it, angst and nervousness filled me.

How will I react to the date that devastated me and left my life shattered?

Yet I found that though I was in a fog and filled with sadness, the trepidation I'd feared didn't manifest itself. I went to the burial site, placed flowers on the grave, and made it through that day without being overwhelmed with sorrow.

When grief is triggered or compounded, it's impossible to know how we'll respond. We believe we've made progress, only to collapse under recurring heartbreak.

For instance, Miles's July birthday was two weeks after the day he died. Since his death, our family has endured another devastating death, my nephew, who was born and passed in July as well. My mother also passed in that month. July has become a dreaded month for which I carry heavy anxiety.

Like me, many grieving people may find it arduous to work through the anxiety and stress of significant milestones. I'm resolving not to place unreasonable demands or expectations on myself or fear the impact of upcoming events. Rather, I'm learning to use them as an opportunity to honor and embrace the memories of my deceased loved ones.

When Grief Unexpectedly Rushes In

While at the grocery store, walking down the aisles, I saw many of Miles's favorite foods. All of a sudden, an onslaught of overwhelming heartache and distress ambushed me. My heart throbbed. I couldn't breathe. I felt the blood coursing through my veins and I rushed to the restroom as tears streamed down my face. After calming myself, I hurried to gather the remaining items on my shopping list and left the store.

Kenzie, a dear family member, had a similar reaction while grocery shopping after her brother passed. "I felt like everything was closing in on me. I couldn't breathe, and I just wanted to get out of there," she shared. "It seemed like almost everything reminded me of my brother."

Without warning, we both experienced a panic attack at the grocery store. Many others have shared how routine tasks they'd performed before their loved one's death now cause them anxiety and dread.

Grief doesn't consult or ask for permission before sneaking up, overtaking, and breaking us down. Panic and distress rush in from out of nowhere and catch us unaware. Neither time nor location dictates those occurrences, and can leave us fleeing or dreading simple errands, daily activities, or routines.

Other people have shared how dread overshadowed them when they went to the grocery store. Prior experiences of seeing someone they know and enduring a barrage of insensitive questions or, on other occasions, not acknowledging them or their loss at all was stressful.

There's no formula to predict everything that might trigger a response. It could be anything and is unique to each individual and relationship. For some, it may happen when we hear a song, visit or pass a certain place, see a friend, or anything that prompts a memory.

I was sitting on the sofa watching TV when a back-to-school commercial came on, highlighting proud parents and excited students packing and heading off to college. Memories of taking Miles to college inundated me with tears.

Regardless of how triggers show up—with or without warning—we can't avoid or eliminate them from our daily lives. As a certified grief educator, I studied with grief expert David Kessler. He said triggers are where the pain lives, and it's also where the healing resides. Developing an awareness of things that trigger us can often provide a guide to determine areas where we can focus our healing.

When we accept the intricacies of bereavement and share our stories, we see how common our experiences are. Then we can free ourselves to move forward in healing by understanding and cooperating with each facet of our journey.

Secondary Losses: Will My Pain Ever End?

When a loved one dies, we not only mourn that person, but as time passes, we grieve the end of plans, hopes, and dreams we held for life with them. In addition, taking on the responsibilities, tasks, and activities they performed, and adjusting to the absence of companionship and resources they provided, prolongs our suffering.

Many people forget about or push aside those secondary losses resulting from the primary death. These are relationship specific and span a broad spectrum—tasks previously performed by the deceased, such as mowing the lawn or cooking meals; observing family traditions and losing hopes and dreams; future plans you held for your loved one or for yourself; and lacking financial stability because your spouse has died.

Grievers may believe these things are too personal to talk about and often choose to remain silent. Some needs may go unsupported by friends and family, while those who grieve are left to struggle alone. Secondary losses make us question if we'll ever get any lasting relief. My heart aches each time I'm reminded of these losses.

I still grieve the hopes and dreams I held for Miles—marriage, fatherhood, success. I'm heartbroken that I'll never be a grandmother, a future event Miles and I talked about often and looked forward to.

I mourn the end of the things he did, like troubleshooting my computer, programming the TV devices, running errands, maintaining my car, and shoveling snow.

When we acknowledge and identify our unique secondary loss areas, we may gain a clearer understanding of grief's complexity and learn how to support ourselves and others with adjusting to and managing life after a loved one dies.

Celebrating while Grieving

Although holidays, other memorable occasions, and daily activities can intensify mourning, they remind us that the love, memories, and space our loved ones held remains in our lives. Expecting and preparing for certain days allows us to develop coping strategies and plan support for the bereaved. Yet we're mindful that we can't always know when or how the intensity of loss might resurface.

I'm learning to allow myself space to tend to my needs. Often, we feel pressured by those who care about us, to do things the way we've always done them, and to act *normal.* They assume that by doing this our sadness will go away. Balancing the differences and demands in family dynamics, such as other children or a surviving parent, may require that some form of normalcy continue; however, the grieving person should have a voice in determining this.

For me, it was the third year into grief before I could decorate for Christmas. I still struggle with holiday cooking. Miles and I had bonded over cooking together and he'd been my taste tester since he was a small boy. I miss our special time.

I'm learning not to commit or force myself to take part in activities if I'm not ready. I still choose to limit myself to small, intimate gatherings with family and friends, but I'm slowly expanding this number.

Connie, a dear family member, had a different experience. She decided to decorate their home and put up a Christmas tree the year her son passed. They had memorial ornaments made and had a small gathering with other immediate family members. She said, "Although I was sad and had to pull away for private moments when I cried, I needed to do that for the rest of the family because we needed to be together."

As we continue to navigate through special days without our transitioned loved ones, we remind ourselves to allow space to grieve. It's a slow process and over time we can learn to acknowledge those dates and seasons through our tears and with family and friends.

When we share the truth about seasons of struggle, we can give and receive support and empathy. This leads to priceless rewards that enable us to build bonds of encouragement and resilience within our community and among family and friends when we need them most.

Moving Forward

Although holidays, other memorable occasions, and daily activities can intensify mourning, these moments remind us that the love, memories, and space our loved ones held in our lives will always remain special. As you experience triggers, be gentle with yourself and remember that triggers are a map of your grief and your healing. Identify your triggers, understand the needs of your pain, and look at the trigger as a conduit for your healing.

CHAPTER 9

Feeling Guilty

Guilt is perhaps the most painful companion of death.
—Coco Chanel

IT WAS MY BIRTHDAY, and I lay in the bed, unable to get up. Heaviness weighted my chest, sadness consumed me, and the tears welling up threatened to spill down my cheeks.

Guilt-laden statements bombarded my thoughts—I had no reason to be happy.

Why should I celebrate my birthday or find joy or happiness when my child is gone?

He'll never get to experience another birthday.

Why am I still alive and he isn't?

I felt guilty for being alive.

Feeling Guilty about Being Happy

Such feelings in mourning generally encompass could, should, would, and why questions. We understand those dilemmas aren't confined only to early months of grief, but can extend into the future and catch us unaware.

I pulled the covers tightly around me and curled into a fetal position. My mind kept turning over, searching for anything that might've sparked the heartache throbbing inside me. I'd had days like that before that related to a significant date or activity. No holiday or triggering milestone came to my mind.

Then it hit me. It had been two-and-a-half years since Miles's death. Bob and I had accepted an invitation to attend a close friend's birthday celebration. We'd gone the previous evening, and for the first time since Miles's passing, I'd allowed myself to have fun. I laughed, danced, and sang, but wished that he'd been there to join in the festivities.

Guilt and remorse threatened to consume me.

How could I have behaved like that?

I'd disrespected Miles's death by my laughing, dancing, and singing.

Will people think I'm not grieving or hurting anymore—that I'm okay?

I felt intense guilt and was paying the price for having enjoyed myself.

Most people probably feel like I did—that we'll never experience genuine joy, laughter, or happiness again. But I've come to understand that grief and happiness can occupy space within me simultaneously. We don't have to choose or deny either the opportunity to exist.

I'm learning to open myself to the possibility that I can celebrate special days without judging myself. I can enjoy the company of others and not be sidelined with sadness afterward.

I'm learning to release the guilt and accept that I'm not betraying Miles by being happy and smiling. Letting go of these feelings allows me to honor my loved one by choosing to embrace the good things that remain and reclaiming my peace.

I'm learning to laugh again. You can too.

Could I Have Done More?

Carrying guilt is a heavy burden. Countless people are holding onto guilty feelings and questioning what they did or didn't do, or wishing they'd done something differently surrounding the death of someone they love. It's often easier to live with guilt than it is to feel helpless about those events. In his *Psychology Today* article, "Guilt, Helplessness, and a Path Forward," psychologist David B. Seaburn challenges us to question if our experiences produce guilt *or* helplessness, if our experiences consist of guilt *and* helplessness. Either way, the two emotions are so closely related that they are interwoven. Could there be things causing these two emotions that we can't change, which leads us to despair?

For most people, if we'd known that the day our person died would have been their last, we would have done many things differently. But we're human and can't know or control every aspect of living and dying.

I should've called the ambulance sooner.

I shouldn't have gone to work.

I should've allowed her to come home.

I should've checked on Dad sooner.

I should've refused to sign that consent form.

The guilt-tripping list is endless.

Noreen was the caregiver for her sister in the latter stages of her cancer journey. Tears streamed down her cheeks when she asked a question that revealed her deepest agony. "I wonder if I could've done more?"

Although Noreen loved her sister dearly, had dedicated herself to caring for her, she still struggled with guilt. "Although my sister assured me she was fine, just tired, I should've recognized something was wrong and called the ambulance sooner."

I could relate to Noreen. I too, carried guilt about Miles's death.

Should I have fought harder to keep him on the ventilator?

Could I have done more to save him?

I'd heard stories of people who, years later, had miraculously emerged from what appeared to be a hopeless situation. Maybe he would've recovered.

I've come to understand that Bob and I made the most unselfish and compassionate decision for our situation and for Miles at that time. I believe God's providence could've performed a miracle for us and for Miles *that day*, and not at some undetermined time in the future if that was how those events were to end.

Guilt only serves to punish and keep us trapped in the past, living with deep pain, and unable to move forward through grief. People look for ways to rationalize why our beloved died, so we ask ourselves questions, hoping to elicit a different outcome than our person dying. We long to believe that we could have saved them. We can't know for sure that doing anything differently would've changed the eventual outcome.

When we seek to identify and examine our guilty feelings surrounding the story we tell ourselves about our loss, then we can uncover the facts about what's *really* true. That's how we begin freeing ourselves from the burden of guilt.

Still, there are cases when someone feels guilty because they believe it *was in their ability* to do more regarding the relationship with their loved one who died.

I didn't help care for Mom like I could have.

I should have allowed the grandchildren to visit more often.

I contributed to drama, stress, and disagreements in the family.

I wasn't there for Dad when he needed me.

These feelings often accompany complicated family dynamics that may cause intense feelings of anger, holding grudges, and blame among family members. When dealing with guilt, at best, we begin releasing those feelings by forgiving ourselves and other people.

Feeling guilty causes us to replay a story of *what if.* We yearn to make sense of death. Our minds want to believe that going back and changing the circumstances might lead to our desired outcome—our loved one wouldn't have died. Doing that means ascribing to ourselves the power to determine life and death.

When we understand that, more often than not, there are diverse facts, chronologies of events leading up to the death, and unknown factors that were out of our control that led to the loss of our person, we realize a single decision or action probably wouldn't have changed the outcome. Finding peace with that releases us from guilt and takes the perceived control out of our hands and places it in the hands of God.

Moving Forward

When we seek to identify and examine those guilty feelings surrounding the story we tell ourselves about our loss, we can then uncover the facts about what's *really* true. That's how we start the process of freeing ourselves from the burden of guilt.

CHAPTER 10

Self-Care while Grieving

*A feeling of pleasure or solace can be so hard to find when you are in
the depths of your grief. Sometimes it's the little things that help get
you through the day. You may think your comforts sound ridiculous
to others, but there is nothing ridiculous about finding one little
thing to help you feel good in the midst of pain and sorrow!*

—Elizabeth Berrien

DURING THE EARLY MONTHS of grief, I struggled to maintain
a balance between my health and wellness—a lifestyle practice
I'd committed to for years. Amid overwhelming devastation, many of
those activities and routines seemed meaningless.

*What benefit are some of those practices, when Miles, a healthy,
vibrant, twenty-six-year-old young man, can suddenly die, without warning?*

My life had shattered, and I knew I couldn't live in such
distraught. I was desperate for relief—something or someone to help
ease the agony of my daily existence. I yearned to escape the cold, cruel,
brutal times of overwhelming grief.

"You've got to cooperate with the season you're in," I'd heard my
pastor and mentor say for years. "Don't fight or run from it; embrace
it and work through it."

I was living the darkest, most devastating time of my life and
her words echoed in my thoughts. I couldn't imagine how I could,
but I knew I couldn't live with that suffering. I longed to know how
others found relief from intense grief.

How do I cooperate with this piercing pain? Is that possible—to embrace my grief and move through it?

Maintaining Balance

Grief hurls our lives off balance, destabilizes us, and is stressful and exhausting. At a time when we're consumed with intense pain, our focus is often limited to just surviving the day. Maintaining balance and practicing self-care isn't an urgent task that most grieving people prioritize. Being unbalanced and neglecting ourselves allows grief and pain to remain trapped inside, and many times leaves the bereaved stuck in grief.

Finding balance allows us to nurture ourselves in healthy ways. When we make our personal needs, health, and care a priority, we give ourselves an opportunity to release stress and pain that our bodies and minds are holding. Incorporating self-care is often a key factor that leads to new ways of embracing life again and moving forward toward healing.

As I would learn, many of us neglect our own needs in grief and rarely show ourselves the same compassion we'd give to someone else. We learn that placing attention on ourselves and focusing on our own needs is selfish. Some even feel guilty or unworthy when considering being compassionate and loving toward themselves. Avoiding our needs during grief can leave us feeling hopeless, which can lead to unhealthy and damaging behaviors, including overindulging in alcohol, using drugs, eating disorders, or breaking social relationships.

Making ourselves a priority takes courage. Self-care demands boldness to respond to the yearning inside by seeking, asking for, and accepting support. I had to learn that focusing on my needs wasn't selfish but an act of love. Neglecting my needs would only keep me in a state of raw pain.

Grief is multi-faceted because every part of us grieves—body, mind, and spirit. Altura Health Systems, a Mayo Clinic Network member, writes about the importance of self-care on its online blog. The article confirms that because grief can be raw and painful, self-care is a key component to the healing process. When we practice self-care, it eases suffering in our mind, body, and spirit. This understanding encourages us to nurture our total being.

Emotional Self-Care

Having excruciating painful emotions is a characteristic of mourning that most grieving people can relate to. That stress casts us into deep despair where we feel lost and hopeless.

Emotional self-care is vital in learning to live with grief and establishing a safe environment where we're supported. Integrating tools that facilitate our ability to manage our day-to-day emotions leads to an increased sense of well-being.

Finding Help

Trusted family and friends who're willing to listen and assist us through grief can be a significant source of emotional comfort. At times, we might seek aid from other sources. Libraries, bookstores, support groups like Tender Hearts, Compassionate Friends, and GriefShare provide and teach emotional self-care during grief. Many churches and religious organizations offer grief classes. You can also find blogs, podcasts, and websites that provide grief resources.

During those early months when I began searching online, I looked for resources to help and for people who could relate with my pain and validate my grievous emotions. Some valuable resources included grief expert David Kessler's website, grief.com, his social media pages interviews, and books, including *Finding Meaning: The Sixth Stage of Grief*, and Megan Devine's book *It's OK That You're Not Okay*. Author Tom Zuba's books *Permission to Mourn* and *Becoming Radiant*, along with his online support group, were instrumental in validating my grief experience and were effective tools that helped me understand my own grief. I found solace among those who hurt as I did. They empowered me to embrace and validate my grief, to find the courage to grieve freely and fully and eventually find meaning in order to move forward.

Later, I learned a valuable lesson about recognizing and establishing emotional boundaries. (The topic of boundaries extends beyond what's covered in this chapter and will be addressed in its own chapter.) While initially useful in early grief, over time, reading and interacting with other people's detailed accounts of excruciating grief kept my pain raw. Some days the distress intensified my grief. I determined that limiting those stories and information gave me relief from a continuous state of emotional overload.

Creating balance and knowing when to embrace or back away from such groups became a catalyst for growth in supporting myself emotionally. Becoming fully present with myself and releasing the mental anguish helped me to clear my mind of some of its cloudiness.

Mental Clarity

Grief envelops many of us in a mental fog and leaves us feeling dazed, disorganized, exhausted, unable to concentrate. We're alarmed when we find the eggs in the pantry or stand in a room wondering, *What did I come in here for?*

For a long time, I felt I was in an alternate universe where nothing was quite right. I was lost, blindly searching through the darkness for a button, a door, an answer—anything to free me from the mental confusion and disarray.

Since then I've spoken to others who shared a similar anxiety.

"I feel like I'm losing my mind. Is there something wrong with me?" they ask.

I reply gently, "No, that's normal. You're grieving."

Finding tools to illuminate the darkness of grief is a vital step in tending our mental well-being. That assists in clearing some of the brain fog and reassures us we *are* sane. For instance, a lot of us find that writing in a journal helps to sort through and release our emotions. Others might listen to soothing music to gain clarity and peace.

In the first year of grief, I was desperate for guidance and information. I purchased books and audio recordings. I read only a couple of those books and scanned the others for relevant information. My attention span was short, and many of the books were too long to hold my focus. Even so, just from what I read or heard, those resources provided valuable information and points of reference to assist me in grief.

Still, sometimes my heartache was so intense that I had to remind myself to breathe. *Exhale. Drop your shoulders. Just breathe.*

Around the one-year mark after Miles's transition, I hired a yoga instructor, who came to my home once a week and taught me pranayama, a deep breathing exercise. I began incorporating that technique into my daily routine and learned to regulate my breathing to release my stress and anxiety.

Shortly after that, I began using meditation applications like Insight Timer, Calm, and others on YouTube that specifically focused on Scripture. Practicing mindfulness calmed my racing thoughts and taught me relaxation and how to focus on the present moment.

Grief-related insomnia is a common symptom. Like many others in early grief, I woke up every night and couldn't get back to sleep. Incorporating yoga and mindfulness as part of my self-care was effective in improving my sleep and clearing the mental fogginess.

Physical Wellness

In her article "When Grief Gets Physical" from *Psychology Today*, Marilyn A. Mendoza, PhD writes that although grief affects our emotions, it also impacts our physical well-being. After the loss of a loved one, people generally experience some type of physical problem during the first six months. Existing conditions are often exacerbated by grief. The physical strain that grief places on our bodies can leave us drained, weak, and sick. We're distressed, we have muscle aches, shortness of breath, palpitations, blood pressure issues, anxiety, digestive issues, weight loss or gain, sleep issues, lack energy, and endure exasperation of existing illnesses and conditions. When grief affects our bodies, exercise is an effective way to release pain and strengthen us physically and mentally. It requires a strong commitment to exercise when we're depressed.

A few weeks after Miles's transition, I tried to force myself to resume my fitness routine and get back in the gym. I'd been an avid fitness and health advocate and read how others found working out was therapeutic after their loss. Yet I couldn't muster the desire to follow through. I'd lost my passion and discovered it took time and patience for me to find my way back to doing many of the things I enjoyed.

Developing and maintaining a consistent practice of caring for our bodies is more challenging for some than others—regardless of one's activity level before loss. Some people need time and patience to regain motivation to restart routines, while others maintain and find those disciplines beneficial.

Al shared that before his son passed, he walked at least three miles most days and maintained that practice after his loss. "Walking helps to clear my head and sort things out," he told me as I joined him for one of his morning walks on the sports track at our alma mater.

A couple of months lapsed before I began short walks in my neighborhood. Gradually, being in the serene outdoors calmed me, and connecting with nature invigorated me. I had gained weight and didn't like how those extra pounds felt or looked on my body. I missed being fit and working out at the gym. I was ready for change but didn't have the level of motivation I'd enjoyed previously. Finally, a year later, I went back to the gym and began working with a personal trainer. When I met with Jason, my trainer, we prayed together, a practice that occurred frequently, and talked about what was going on in my life, what my goals were. I told him that I needed something to motivate me to stay focused, train on days I wouldn't want to, and remain committed to the program. He encouraged me to train for a fitness competition and dedicate my debut show to Miles.

"That's it!" I said. I had found the motivating force and passion to focus on my physical well-being.

Working out bolstered my energy, and my body became stronger and healthier. I still had challenges with pushing through on milestone dates, holidays, and those unexpected times when grief hit me hard. But I persevered. I found I could grieve and maintain my physical health at the same time. Focusing on my physical well-being facilitated my return to healthier eating habits that were consistent with my body's needs. I eliminated fast foods, sugar, and sodas. I replaced fried foods with baked or grilled. I ate on a schedule and alternated between eating a clean diet, free of hormones and unhealthy additives, and eating vegan.

When grieving, some of us begin emotionally eating, while others lose their appetite. In either situation, when our bodies aren't getting the nutrition needed, intense grief can linger and lead to serious health issues.

Being patient with myself and taking small steps led to me regaining a healthy lifestyle. I experienced days where my grief was intense or I had grief triggers and needed and received compassionate support from my trainer and from myself. But over time I learned that I could hurt and persevere, moving forward. My patience was rewarded as I took the stage as a fit, healthy, and grieving athlete, having earned trophies in four of the five categories in which I competed.

"Gwendolyn dedicates this show to her son, Miles, and thanks her Lord and Savior Jesus Christ," the emcee said as he read the dedication I'd written for the competition.

Spiritual Well-Being

Maintaining my spiritual life was the most crucial aspect in sustaining a practice of self-care and finding relief while living with grief. The agony of Miles's death was so intense I believed that if I didn't cling to my faith, I'd slip further into darkness and would never find my way back. My spiritual life sustained me.

Connection to Faith Community and Prayer

Listening to encouraging sermons and messages reminded me of God's love, which strengthened my soul. My faith community that allowed me to mourn freely and without judgment embraced and supported me. For months, tears flowed down my face as I participated in worship with my church family. I prayed. Sang. Cried.

Sometimes my daily practice of praying became a challenge, and I could only whisper a few words. Some days, I couldn't say anything. At those times, I believed my prayers flowed through my moans and tears. Knowing that others were praying for me carried me through those dark days. Over time, consistently practicing my faith renewed my hope, relieved the intensity of my pain, and enabled me to move forward and reach out to others.

Asking for Support

An aspect of self-care some people shun is the willingness to ask others for help. That's often difficult because grievers don't want to bother anyone, appear weak, or they may think others are too busy. They feel abandoned, forgotten, and sometimes resentful.

Grievers shut out others when they aren't forthcoming about their needs. I've learned there are people who genuinely want to provide support in any way they can. There's a balance we should reach for; that is, knowing when we need to be alone to work with our grief and when acknowledging times of receiving support from family, friends, and others would be beneficial to our well-being.

Professional Counseling

A few months after Miles passed, I determined it might be beneficial to talk with a professional therapist about living with my excruciating loss. I believed I needed to consider whatever options that might help me survive the life I'd now live. I needed to release the emotions and thoughts of my loss in a safe environment. The responsibility of caring for my grieving family, being the administrator of Miles's estate, and taking care of all the unexpected daily tasks weighed heavily on me. Once I found someone with whom I was comfortable, I began grief counseling. Those one-on-one sessions were instrumental in understanding my grieving process and developing coping strategies.

Others shared additional therapies that helped during their loss. One that I found impactful was *Splankna*—a Christian therapy for mind-body psychology that uses the same system in the body in which acupuncture and chiropractic are based. It clears emotional trauma that is physically stored and helps identify where the body is holding different emotions related to root traumas.

Learning to manage our grief begins with small steps. When we accept responsibility for self-care, we progress, our grief changes, and over time we begin to feel better. Incorporating resources and practices that nurture our individual needs can determine how we move through grief and give us the ability to use healthy coping strategies to enhance our total well-being. Adjusting to a new normal of being compassionate, gentle, and patient with ourselves brings healing. When we focus on our well-being while enduring loss, we build resilience.

Moving Forward

While there's a balance we should strive for, it's beneficial to recognize when we need support from family, friends, and others—and when we need to practice self-care.

CHAPTER 11

Boundaries and Relationships

*Daring to set boundaries is about having the courage to
love ourselves even when we risk disappointing others.*

—Brené Brown

WHEN WE NEGLECT TO establish parameters that communicate our needs and desires in grief other people may feel free to impose what they believe is best for you, and often what benefits themselves.

Caring for ourselves and creating a space that's conducive to our healing involves setting limits around what's acceptable and tolerable. We define roles and expectations for relationships with family, friends, and others around our grief. This demands an expanded role of self-care, and boundaries are a catalyst to practicing effective parameters.

Boundaries are guidelines, limits, or rules we set for ourselves and for our relationships so other people know what's acceptable or comfortable for us within those relationships. Dr. Henry Cloud says to think of boundaries as a property line that identifies the borders of where what's acceptable to us begins and ends. Even outside the complexities of grief, setting boundaries can be one of life's unpleasant necessities because many people struggle to set and honor boundaries.

Most, if not all, of us think that if we set a boundary that honors ourselves, it will come across as selfish or rude; and we don't want to appear selfish. We neglect our well-being by overcommitting ourselves, overextending ourselves, and doing things to avoid conflict or making other people uncomfortable. So we resort to people pleasing, abandoning our needs and intentions, and placing other people's opinions and desires above our own. We internalize this behavior as our way of sacrificial living; however, setting boundaries is practicing and maintaining self-care and self-preservation.

Establishing healthy boundaries is even more challenging during grief when we're vulnerable and hurting and need the support of family and friends. Many people doubt they have the courage, energy, or patience to set limits that benefit their own physical, emotional, mental, and physical well-being. Responsibilities and decisions we previously performed and logically evaluated have become chaotic and overwhelming, especially since our brains are foggy with grief.

Yet in our pain, we strive to live up to expectations placed on us by others, as well as those we place on ourselves. We fear losing anyone else or valued relationships in our lives and surrender to silence rather than listen to internal alarms and warnings. And, as we will learn in this chapter, failing to show up for ourselves and set a boundary can lead to feelings of anger, anxiety, discomfort, fear, guilt, offense, stress, and resentment.

Setting Boundaries

When I was growing up, my grandmother said, "Child, say what you mean and mean what you say." Ask for what you want and don't keep changing your mind. If you say yes, mean yes, and if you say no, mean no.

It may be harder to say no or speak up for yourself when you're hurting emotionally and aren't thinking as clearly. In her book *Set Boundaries, Find Peace: A Guide to Reclaiming Yourself*, therapist Nedra Glover Tawwab explains that to effectively interact with others when setting boundaries, it's important to know when to say yes, and when saying no is best. Showing up for yourself by setting boundaries can protect you when you're bereaved and feel weak. This requires a level of self-awareness and an ability to identify and clearly state our needs and acceptable limits around different relationships at various times and in specific situations.

Being able to say, "Today I need time alone," or "For now, I need you to leave my mother's belongings where they are," helps us maintain control over areas in our lives during a time when grief makes us feel powerless.

Saying, "Thank you for asking. I'd rather not talk about that," when someone talks about a subject you aren't comfortable with honors your conversational boundaries, and, "That's a kind gesture, but please check with me before doing something on my behalf, or making a business decision that involves me," protects your decision-making boundaries. Something like, "Please come to me with questions or anything that may impact my children," is an example of a boundary in which someone felt their parenting decisions were violated.

When boundaries are violated, grieving people may feel disrespected or bitter over loss of control in their life, time, or situation. Their grief may be intensified.

If you feel that the person who is supporting you continues to overstep or violate your personal limits, you could respond with love and with a consequence, such as, "I love you dearly and want you in my life, but if you insist on asking prying questions about the details of my father's death, I'll have to limit my conversations with you. I hope you understand this is very painful for me to talk about right now."

Honoring the bereaved's boundaries is an empathic act that communicates respect for their wishes and supports their effort to maintain control, timing, and emotional tolerance over the identified area where guidelines are set. Staying within those limits helps to minimize their stress and pain, and reduces the strain on relationships and aids in healing.

When we're grieving or even setting the smallest limit, recognizing when other people don't respect or follow our limits is important. Sometimes others may misunderstand what our boundaries are.

To set a boundary, your words need to be clear in what you want and what you need. The words we use need to be specific, kind, and direct. Nedra Glover Tawwab stresses in her book *Set Boundaries, Find Peace: A Guide to Reclaiming Yourself* that when we're clear in communicating our boundaries, we've put ourselves in a position to save our relationships.

To communicate plainly in any circumstance in life, we need to *know* ourselves and the limits of how we need to be treated and what we're willing to tolerate. This includes being slow to agree or disagree on a matter without considering the present or future outcome of our decision.

Sometimes grieving people aren't clear about what they need or want from people; therefore, other people aren't sure about those needs or wants. Once we establish a boundary around something, others are better equipped to respect and follow through on those wishes.

Relationships Change

When a person is in a bereaved situation, some relationships may change or shift to a different frequency. In the grieving stage, there are instances where contact and socializing is paused. Being supportive and understanding under these situations gives the bereaved freedom and time to grieve as they need. They will know when they are ready to reengage with family and friends. Sometimes though, because the grieving person has set limits for how much they engage with others or what they can and cannot talk about, they risk jeopardizing their relationships.

Even so, relationships have a better likelihood of staying intact when boundaries are set and clearly communicated, and then respected and followed by those for whom they were set, and enforced.

The risk comes when, as a result of speaking up for ourselves and identifying what's not acceptable, people will treat us differently, become offended, or even pull away or end a relationship. Like Katherine had experienced (from chapter 7), it's difficult to watch how others choose to react to our difficult but necessary personal boundaries with people we love and care about. Furthermore, Katherine says,

What disappointed me the most was the change in my relationship with some of my Christian brothers and sisters. It broke my heart even more when they distanced themselves from me, as if to imply that God was punishing me for some evil deed or sin I'd committed. I never knew that someone's death could make people behave like that. I never knew I'd lose friends.

Risks, Establishing Boundaries, and Talking about What Hurts

When I was in the midst of my mourning, I had to become honest about my pain. I wanted others to be aware of the words and actions that hurt me. I've been able to show up for myself by showing through my actions and teaching others how to communicate with me.

This didn't come without risks. About six months after Miles died, I lost a relationship with a close family member when I respectfully told him that the words he spoke to me after Miles's transition were insensitive and hurtful. He became defensive and offended because I didn't agree with his opinion about my disappointment or see things his way.

When establishing boundaries with those we know personally, the risk is greater for unintentional offenses to harm relationships. Thoughts of losing or straining relationships provoke anxiety and fear, which tend to push us to choose to sacrifice our emotional and mental well-being for the sake of maintaining our friendships. We would rather put up with offensive or insensitive behavior. Yet once we realize the harm done to ourselves because of our weak boundaries, we learn to eliminate potentially discouraging dialogue. We learn that we can communicate more effectively with people who want to help us.

For almost five years, I tried to reestablish that relationship, but my family member didn't want to reconnect. I've decided to respect his decision and move forward, knowing that I'm stronger because I did what was right for my own grieving heart.

Sometimes when we, as the bereaved, set a limit or boundary with someone who did not respect that boundary, we might reach out and initiate communication in order to salvage that relationship. However, because the person didn't respect our limits, they might choose not to engage with us. And as such, the relationship is broken.

"I was the disrespected person, but I'm the one reaching out to her," Pamela says, referring to the broken relationship she had with her cousin. "She's mad at me, refuses to answer my calls, and won't respond to my texts or voice messages." She shrugged her shoulders and shook her head sadly. "I've decided to let it go and move past it."

Sometimes when establishing boundaries, some people will become offended and break off the relationship because they may not understand the full reason for that boundary or limit. Dr. Henry Cloud says in his book *Boundaries* that just because someone gets mad or says they're hurt doesn't mean you shouldn't set boundaries. Being *responsible to* the other persons and considering the possible effects is something you consider when setting boundaries. When people do not understand our words or our actions, it's helpful to remember the reason why we set the boundary, which is a consequence of other people crossing our boundary line. If they pull away from us, then over time, restoring the relationship might be possible; however, we need to be mindful that it may not, for many reasons we may or may not understand. This might feel uncomfortable and hard for us because we can't control what other people do. In the end, our growth and well-being are what's important.

Many times deep hurt occurs when boundaries are disrespected and relationships end or cause other damaging consequences. Deciding not to talk to a bereaved person or listen to their wishes after they set a boundary shows disrespect for their feelings and can be harmful to both parties. Getting upset or angry because a boundary has been set can be an indication that limits were needed in that area.

Although the book *I Want This to Work: An Inclusive Guide to Navigating the Most Difficult Relationship Issues We Face in the Modern Age* is directed to couples, it is relevant to other relationships during the grief process. Therapist Elizabeth Earnshaw shares that a boundary seeks to maintain a current relationship, not to hurt or harm you or the relationship.

When people add stress, drain our energy, or disrespect us, bearing the weight of that relationship becomes problematic and unhealthy.

We shrink back and tolerate offensive and insensitive behavior and make decisions that aren't in our best interest.

While most grieving people need and ask for help or advice from those in their support system, some individuals see this as an opportunity to direct and dictate how someone should grieve. They may see mourning people as vulnerable, weak, and unable to manage their lives and affairs. They think they're helping us and know what's best for our situation. Although they respond out of concern and compassion, speaking up for ourselves and setting rules and limits around that behavior can strain those relationships also.

When we talk with people about our boundaries, and they aren't agreeable and choose to disrespect us, it may become necessary to pull away or limit our time with them in order to maintain an environment that supports our grief journey.

That's not always possible in relationships among immediate family, including spouses, partners, parents, children, siblings, and grandparents. In addition, other present issues often strain these relationships, such as feeling too much responsibility being placed on one individual, people not pulling their weight, not being supported, or failing to meet or being present for another person in a way they need. Working through these issues may require the help of a professional counselor or spiritual adviser. But, understanding that each person is grieving in their own way and has their own needs gives us space to evaluate, honor, and validate their process rather than judge or compare it to our own.

Grief changes us and it changes others, and there will be times and situations when we won't know why we lost relationships with people after the death of someone we love. Some people can't walk, sit with, or accompany us on our grief journey. Accepting that frees us and them from the burden of painful expectation and disappointment. Yet it challenges us to examine the emotional territory where others are most likely to cross.

Common Boundaries

Each individual determines areas where limits need to be placed around their loss. When we're grieving, talking with someone we trust can help us determine areas where limits need to be set, valid concerns of where and when someone is crossing our boundaries, or when we can get help with ways to establish boundaries or stick to or enforce them.

Some common areas that may require limits include the following:

Personal. We set these for ourselves to ensure we meet our needs in a healthy way. For example, insisting that others respect our privacy.

Relationship. These guidelines dictate agreed-upon limits with family, friends, or coworkers.

Conversational. We determine what topics we're comfortable talking about, when, and with whom.

Emotional. Within these boundaries, we give ourselves permission to feel emotions without allowing other people to guide or judge us.

Financial. These limits reduce the risks of someone taking advantage of us or our financial responsibilities and support.

Physical. Whether setting parameters around personal space, time, or reclaiming a peaceful space to grieve, these limits give us a sense of control over our space. They might address someone touching us in uncomfortable ways, or even people coming into our home and rearranging our belongings or removing items without permission.

When we learn to follow and honor the limits we set for ourselves, most people will respect our needs; however, some people will not fully understand our boundaries.

Common Unhelpful Reactions from Others

The purpose of this section is to provide examples of common reactions someone may exhibit when boundaries are imposed. This helps the grieving person examine and reflect on how we might respond to set guidelines.

Hurtful and unhelpful reactions often sprout from the consequences of others crossing our boundaries. Those feelings don't benefit our efforts to move forward.

Justification is when someone has abused a boundary and offers a self-approved rationale or opinion for crossing that line. For example, the supporting person might say, "Well, I'm trying to help you. I thought you'd be happy that I asked the ladies to stop by to clean your mother's bedroom."

Disregard ignores and does not *hear* what the grieving person is saying. The person trying to offer support does not respect the griever's needs and wishes and actually discounts them.

Anger occurs when someone becomes deeply offended by an imposed boundary, which often results in the relationship becoming distant or broken. It can also point to the violator's inability to set or enforce boundaries in their own lives.

Blame comes from not taking responsibility for accepting or respecting a boundary. Blame also projects the lack of accountability onto the person who's grieving or onto someone else.

As the grieving person, we support our healing journey when we resist the urge to accept blame for other people's actions and do not blame them for ours. Conversely, when supporters imagine themselves as the grieving person, they can become empathetic and sensitive to the needs and challenges of living with the death of a loved one. They're able to better understand the bereaved's need for boundaries. Respecting boundaries shows your support and compassionate heart toward helping the bereaved person.

Though you can't control how the other person responds, you can modulate your response by speaking the truth in love and showing grace, which contributes to having peace of mind when dealing with disappointing responses.

Extending Grace

Most people who show up for us do so with an intention to help and support. Sometimes we expect others to know what to say to us, what we need from them, or how to respond to our grief. But in most instances, people don't know or understand unless *we tell them*. We can expect people will cross boundaries, and such affronts as insensitive words or conversations, inconsiderate acts, gestures, or suggestions might anger, hurt, or offend us.

We can't expect that people will always know where we are on our grief journey or understand the ongoing challenges of living with the death of a loved one. Although it may be difficult for us to communicate, it's still our responsibility.

Be willing to extend grace to people. Grace treats others with kindness, leniency, compassion, concern, and sympathy, even when they inadvertently say or do hurtful things. Extending grace is necessary and important when maintaining relationships. During those times, I remind myself that we've all said and done unintentional things that hurt or offended someone. Others will do the same to us. That's why I first seek to extend the same grace to others as others have shown toward me. This doesn't mean that we compromise or allow people to disrespect us, but we give space for people to be human, learn, and grow alongside us.

Moving Forward

Learning to trust the value of setting boundaries helps us validate and respect ourselves and others. Trusting our boundaries are in place to enable us to care for ourselves and keep us safe, gives us and others space to grow and heal as we honor ourselves and our journey.

CHAPTER 12

Grief and the Digital Era

Because grief is so isolating and social connections are such a major part of healing from loss, having a public component to grieving rituals— gatherings, reminiscing, bringing over food—is common across cultures.

—Rachel Hutton

"I SAT FROZEN IN place with my eyes locked on the phone screen. Anxiety rushed through my body and I inhaled a gulp of air," Lynn recounted. "I wasn't expecting to see Chris's smiling face staring back at me."

She'd been startled when a picture of her son appeared on her social media timeline. Her son's friend had posted the photo, honoring his memory and saying how much he missed him.

"I didn't know if I should feel happy or sad," she said.

Social Media Mourning

Social media platforms like Facebook, Instagram, YouTube, and other applications used to connect and share information are changing how we interact and mourn with family and friends when loss occurs. They're a source of support, collective grief, and community during tough times and seasons, and a means of normalizing grief within society.

Online posts can also spark inner turmoil, may seem intrusive, and often become triggers to those in early grief. For some people, it creates a sense of *loss of control* over the comments, posts, unexpected pictures, memorial pages, friend suggestions, or other reminders of their loved ones that appear online.

"I was fighting mad when an acquaintance posted on Facebook, before my family had a chance to, that my sister had died," Michelle said as we sat on her sofa two days after her sister passed. "We hadn't even notified all of our family members about her passing when I began getting calls, and text messages. Some of our close family members and friends learned on Facebook that she had died."

Like Michelle, other people have shared their anger and feelings on how they had been disrespected when someone else announced the death of their loved one on social media *before* they did. Such acts tend to be viewed as insensitive. Friends and acquaintances should be cautioned against undertaking such actions before the family has published the announcement.

"When I saw my sister's face as someone else's profile picture, I was conflicted and didn't know how I felt about that," Bryan said to my husband, Bob, and me during our visit to his home. "I came to accept that I can't control what other folks post, but it's good to know they're thinking about her."

For other people, like Bryan, these kinds of actions provide a means to communicate and share information with a larger group at once. Notifications of loss and the resulting grief, while previously confined to a smaller, more intimate group of family and friends, are now shared with thousands of people with a push of a button on our computer or cell phone. It's often a result of how many people learn of someone's death.

When Miles passed, I used social media to notify those outside of immediate family and close friends of his transition. It was one of the hardest announcements I'd ever made as I garnered all the courage and strength, typed the announcement of his death, and posted on Facebook. In the days that followed, I provided updates regarding the Celebration of Life service and where memorial acknowledgments and contributions could be sent.

An outpouring of condolences and support flooded my timeline. Calls, text messages, and other acts of support followed as people read that post. In the years since his passing, posting on social media has helped me to share my grief journey with others, support other grieving people, and receive support.

Multitudes of people use social media to express their reality of living with loss. Talking about loved ones, sharing stories, memories and tributes, giving and receiving support, and sharing their most vulnerable pain has a positive effect and is often instrumental in the healing process.

In the digital era, grieving isn't without pitfalls. Just as some might be uncomfortable with seeing people grieve in person, this same discomfort and resistance to change extends in the online spaces. Live streaming funerals and memorial services have become a widely accepted practice, integrating online accommodations into the traditional mourning process. Many see it as beneficial for those unable to attend services in person and a practice that's here to stay.

Memorial Fundraising and Insensitive Behavior

When Denise passed away, her sorority sisters rallied around her family and organized an online fundraising page where friends contributed money to assist with expenses associated with her loss.

"Her friends were a big blessing to us," her parents, James and Darlene, said. "They set up a page where people could donate money. It covered a lot of expenses and took away the financial strain we otherwise may have had."

Clara, a single mother, had a different experience after her son passed. Two of her son's friends contacted her to let her know they'd organized a giving campaign in her son's memory and would present the proceeds to her.

"A lot of our friends want to make a donation in DeShawn's name," one young man told her.

"We're organizing it and will make sure you get the money," another said.

Weeks later she had not received any donations, so Clara called one of the friends, who informed her she'd receive the money within the week. Clara continued checking with them over the following months until they stopped accepting her calls. She never received the money from the fundraiser.

"I just stopped calling," she said, sitting across the conference room table from me while putting together notebooks for a meeting. "It hurts me to know they used my son's death to take advantage of me and other people," she said with tears in her eyes.

"Are you going to reach out to some of the other friends in their circle and let them know that you never received the money?" I asked.

"No, I'm going to leave it alone." She wiped away a tear. "I'm hurting too much to deal with that right now. I'll leave it in God's hands."

The generosity of people to donate money and resources to help those who are grieving is almost automatic and one of the greatest acts of kindness during loss. However, both donors and grievers should be careful to ensure that donated funds are collected and dispersed by reputable people and organizations.

Occasionally, other displays of insensitive behavior occur online by trolls and people who make prying, embarrassing, or inappropriate comments or jokes online about the deceased or family that are upsetting. While we may remove some comments and the person who posted it may take it down, the harm has already happened. That's a risk of interacting on social media and most of us have witnessed it on some level. Online grief isn't exempted. When this happens, it may be helpful to pull away from social media for a while.

The Choice Is Yours

Choosing how often we interact on social media and use online platforms while grieving is a very personal decision. It's also important to remember that there's no right or wrong reaction to online triggers and it's normal for reactions to change over time and it's okay to react differently to each event.

For most of us, it can bring comfort knowing that, whether online or offline, memories of our loved ones live in the hearts and thoughts of family and friends. Connecting online, having grief witnessed by others, and allowing them into our grief is an integral step toward healing.

Our loved one's digital footprint—social media pages, websites, posts, pictures, and other content—remain active and will continue to be a part of our lives. While seeing posts about our loved one may be painful, they become a trove of treasured memories. Like their digital footprint, our love for them is a tribute and reminder that can't be erased.

Moving Forward

Talking about loved ones, sharing stories, memories and tributes, giving and receiving support, and sharing their most vulnerable pain has a positive effect, and is often instrumental in the healing process.

PART 3
Moving Forward

CHAPTER 13

Messages, Signs, and Symbols

*Perhaps they are not the stars in the sky, but rather openings
where our loved ones shine down to let us know they are happy.*

—Eskimo Proverb

THE DEATH OF SOMEONE close to us leaves a gaping, agonizing emptiness inside. Every day their absence reminds us of how much we miss them. We think about the space they held in our lives and yearn for something familiar and meaningful to reassure us they're still a part of our life.

We value belongings that hold special memories—a favorite t-shirt, jewelry, letters, pictures, and mementos. Those treasures help us feel connected and fill some of the void. But for multitudes of people, the connection with their loved ones extends beyond these possessions when we receive affirmations that confirm a continuous bond after their transition.

God speaks to us through messages, signs, and symbols to bring us comfort and peace. These encounters tend to encourage and strengthen us as we move forward on our grief journey.

Such beliefs or events are sometimes discounted or frowned upon, and some people suggest that those living with grief should dismiss such incidents because they claim those events are only coincidences or have no significant meaning.

For some of us, our faith cautions against practices that go contrary to religious teachings. But for these unsolicited messages, signs, and symbols we must determine if they're acceptable or not. I've found that acknowledging such beliefs and accounts doesn't contradict what I believe spiritually. Those unexpected experiences occur during our daily activities. They tend to bring tranquility, healing, and renew or sustain our hope to move forward through loss.

Comfort and Solace

Millions of people attest that they too have found solace in receiving such affirmations. Messages, signs, and symbols can express themselves in many ways and are unique to our relationship with our loved one. They can manifest themselves in common occurrences that leave us with a sense of peace and contentment.

Some of us have dreams, sense the presence, or smell a familiar fragrance or aroma of our loved one. We connect through nature when we see a rainbow cascading across the sky, a blooming flower, special birds, feathers, or a colorful butterfly that lingers or lands close by. We might receive messages, signs, and symbols when we hear a special song, find a letter or card from the loved one, and receive comfort from our pet's behavior, some precious object, or anything that holds a special memory.

For most of my life, I've believed these events were possible. As a child, I had heard my grandmother and others speak about those affirmations. Before Miles passed, I hadn't experienced anything that confirmed their significance or reality. After his transition, I felt lost and filled with hopeless pain. I longed to see and hug him again and yearned to feel his presence and know he was okay.

"God, please give me something to ease my pain," I prayed.

About a month after he'd transitioned, I dreamed about Miles. It was so lifelike—a divine visitation. I still remember details about the intense love and joy that filled me. I felt greatly comforted and relieved to hold my child in my arms, hug, and talk with him.

When I awoke, I knew we'd been together.

That visitation in my dream carried greater meaning because it occurred on the morning of my birthday. Though I had grieved deeply that day, the comfort received from that event was an answer to prayer.

While some people might accept those signs as insignificant or coincidental, for many of us who grieve, we interpret these kinds of dreams as divine connections with our deceased loved ones.

Over the next two years, I experienced three other visitations. Those special encounters gave me hope and encouraged me during some of my most desperate and despairing times. Not only did I find solace in dreams, but I found solace in other signs as well.

In the beginning, I frequently visited the memorial gardens where Miles is laid to rest. Each day as I drove there, I noticed the beautiful flowers planted beside the road. Their beauty calmed and consoled me. After a while I stopped going as often, but I still thought of the flowers. I didn't know their name so I took pictures. Later, I went online and researched the plant. Then one day, I found it—the hibiscus.

The next summer I planted hibiscus in the flowerbed outside my front door. During the following year, I watched their growth closely. July was ending, and it didn't appear that the flowers would bloom. I had a one-day trip planned and walked outside to check the flowerbed before I left. Still no blooms. When I returned home the next day—Miles's birthday—one flower was in full bloom with a big, beautiful, red blossom. My face burst into a beaming smile, my heart filled with joy, and I believed the blooming flower held a personal message for me.

Heavenly Smile

Other people have shared stories of signs that eased their pain and strengthened them on their grief journey. Ten years after his nineteen-year-old son passed, George continued to struggle with his loss, living with deep emotional pain. Like George, others face struggles even when it's been a long time since the deceased has been gone. "I looked good on the outside," he commented, "but inside I was torn up."

George couldn't find peace, his faith was constantly being battered, and he'd started making bad personal decisions trying to fill the void left by his loss.

After facing the consequences of yet another bad decision, George knew he couldn't continue to live with the deep despair and questions that tormented him about the sudden and traumatic death of his son. He longed for something from God that would ease his agony and help him move forward in his grief.

"I needed to get to the bottom of this," he said.

That's when he began counseling with his pastor. One day during a raw and transparent counseling session, George lamented his anguish, frustration, and longing for God to bring him closure and relief about his son's death.

His pastor prayed, "God, show George what you want him to know about his son."

In that moment, sitting in the office with his head bowed and eyes closed, George saw a vision. "It was as if God pulled a veil back. I saw my son's face smiling down at me from above. He said, 'Hi, Daddy.'"

Then George heard a voice, an impression from God. "He's with me."

The message George received that day released him from tormenting pain he'd endured for ten years and gave him the comfort and freedom to move forward and embrace life again.

My Brother's Keeper

We all hold diverse beliefs about signs, symbols, and messages. While some grieving people may find this experience helpful, it's acknowledged that others might not have such an experience.

I'd prayed daily that God would comfort my older son, RL, who is differently abled and has special needs. I asked him to answer in a special way and help RL process Miles's death. RL had lost his brother and his best friend.

About a month after Miles's transition, RL came home from work at the grocery store. We walked downstairs to the basement, which he and his brother had shared, and sat down on the loveseat.

"I know you're sad and hurt really bad and you miss Miles," I said. "I want you to know that you can talk to Miles and tell him what you're feeling. I talk to him all the time."

"I know, Mom," he said. "Miles has already talked to me." RL got up from the chair, stood directly in front of me, looked me in my eyes, and shared this story.

A few days prior, RL was at work in the parking lot gathering shopping carts, when he felt someone touch his shoulder. "I turned around but didn't see anyone. Then I heard Miles's voice, saying, 'We've been together our whole lives, and we're inseparable. Although you can't see me, I'm always by your side. You're not alone; you can always talk to me.' He said although I was sad now, he wanted me to move forward in life."

I believe that supernatural encounter provided consolation to RL and eased his sorrow.

Such experiences powerfully impact our lives. They remind us that love and relationship remain with those who've passed. Though our beloveds are no longer with us physically, we'll always be connected, spirit to spirit—the part of us that lives forever. This is my understanding and interpretation, and I respect that it might not be yours. For myself, holding such beliefs provides comfort to me and my family in our grief because we know that our loved one is safe with God.

We can't completely understand the diverse manifestations of incidents, mysteries, and miracles many of us experience after the death of someone we love. But if acknowledging those experiences lifts our spirit, brings joy and peace, we can give ourselves permission to embrace those things that speak to our hearts and bring healing to our souls.

Relationship Lives On

Even though death ends a physical relationship, it doesn't have to annul the bond which connects us to the person who transitioned. Many suggest that the deepest essence of our internal self or spiritual nature lives on. We remain connected to those who've passed, spirit to spirit, meaning that the love we shared—memories and unique life experiences—binds us together, keeping our departed loved ones alive in our hearts. When I affirmed the belief that my own relationship with Miles and others' relationship with Miles continues in differ-ent ways, I became hopeful that I could move forward and embrace life again.

Many long to know and seek assurance that our beloveds are still with us and that progressing in life after loss doesn't mean we forget them. When we sense them or see something that reminds us of them, we can feel both pain and joy. The ache of missing them might cause tears of sadness to well up, but knowing that they're with us can brighten our countenance with a smile. Those connections may prick our hearts but still provide comfort. They remind us that although they have died, our love hasn't.

It's not uncommon for those who've experienced loss to experience a deep sense of connection when they talk to their loved one. I feel the impact of both love and loss each time I say, "Good morning," or "Good night, Miles," "I miss you," or "I know that was from you," when something happens that reminds me of my loved one who passed.

Understanding that we carry our beloveds forward—not leave them in the past—ignites hope, eases the pain of grief, and helps release apprehension to engaging in life. Embracing memories, sharing stories, and observing former and new rituals sustains the love and relationship with our beloveds. Allowing ourselves the freedom to experience that connection is a gift of love that strengthens our heart, mind, and spirit.

Because our love continues, our relationship continues.

Moving Forward

While death ends a physical relationship, we can move forward and appreciate the memories, comfort, and support from others, know-ing our loved ones are okay, and that our own grief is valid.

CHAPTER 14

When We Hurt Deeply

Deep grief sometimes is almost like a specific location, a coordinate on a map of time. When you are standing in that forest of sorrow, you cannot imagine that you could ever find your way to a better place. But if someone can assure you that they themselves have stood in that same place, and now have moved on, sometimes this will bring hope.

—Elizabeth Gilbert

"GOD, WILL I HURT this badly for the rest of my life? Will I always be this sad and ache for my child so intensely?"

During the early years following loss, many of us can't imagine a time when the intensity of our pain will soften. We won't wake up one day with our pain gone. But as time passes, we adapt to life with our loved ones and our grief changes. The piercing heartache eases and becomes lighter to carry.

When we create stories around our loss, the inner dialogue we have with ourselves is often the source of intense pain. From my Grief Educator Certification class notes, David Kessler says that people in grief create stories around their loss. This is neither good nor bad. But when they connect to a story that is not true and is not helpful, they can get stuck in the narrative.

We tell ourselves stories about ourselves. A widow might say, "I can never take care of the house on my own." Someone whose child died might say, "There is no way I can ever smile again." It's important to note that sometimes the story can be true, and yet we have to realize it's still a story.

Each day as I fought through the unpredictable emotions of living with loss, I doubted I'd ever arrive at that place. I longed to believe the future held relief for me and prayed it would. Over time, I realized that the death of a loved one didn't mean being sentenced to a lifetime of suffering. I accepted that grieving my loss was necessary to move forward, and I needed to recognize and observe how I engaged with and responded to my grief. I began to understand that some of the painful thoughts I had held about Miles's death and my lost dreams for his future only amplified my heartache and led to hopelessness.

When we repeat agonizing stories to ourselves, they intensify our pain, keep us in distress, and trap us in a cycle of suffering. Focusing on the "What-ifs" and "If-onlys" only fuels our anxiety and steals our peace. We're unable to receive the comfort and relief necessary to move forward.

I learned I have a choice of determining my inner dialogue and how I respond to the distressing thoughts when they come. Some days, even now, grief weighs heavily, and I must be present with it and surrender to the attention it demands. But on other days, I'm learning to reframe my confusing and painful thoughts to bring comfort and peace.

I decided to make grief my ally, instead of fearing it or allowing it to hold me captive. I assigned purpose to my pain and began to honor my loved ones by choosing to live and carry their memories forward.

While we feel pain, sadness, loneliness, fear, and uncertainty—natural responses to loss—each of us gets to decide if long-term suffering will become the reality of our future. In our decision, we're able to recognize and understand the impact of those distressful thoughts, we can change how we respond to them mentally, emotionally, and spiritually. Glimmers of hope break through the darkness, and we experience gentler days when we change our internal dialogue and free ourselves from suffering.

Searching for Hope

The agony of losing someone we love causes us to doubt whether our life has meaning or purpose. When our heart's broken, joy's gone, and passion for life is drained, thoughts about the future appear dismal. We're downhearted, dejected, and it's difficult to be hopeful.

What's there to look forward to?

We stumble through the darkness of grief, pained by reminders of unfulfilled expectations, shattered dreams, and shaken confidence, which leave us empty, helpless, lonely, and disillusioned. We keep those feelings to ourselves and a sense of hopelessness overtakes us.

After Miles passed, I became accustomed to existing daily without encouraging expectations for the future. I struggled through periods when I doubted my life had meaning or that I'd ever be happy. Many days hopelessness engulfed me, and I embraced it. It seemed right to do. My child had died. What enjoyment could life give? None, I believed.

I yearned to know that someday I'd regain hope to live a purposeful life. I believed I owed that to Miles's memory. As time passed, that belief compelled me to confront my anxiety, doubts, and fears, which pushed me to move forward.

I learned that other hurting people also remain silent and alone in their hopelessness. I came to understand that is a common response to grief, and I could share those feelings with others who experienced the same. I inquired, listened, and read other people's stories. Seeing grieving people regain hope and a desire to live again led me to consider whether there was a way out of feeling hopeless for me.

Is it possible to embrace life and find happiness again?

I learned that regaining hope would require effort, and commitment, and I opened myself to discover a new "What if?" A tiny seed planted inside me, and faint rays of hope pricked my heart. I became willing to take a chance, trust, and believe that life might still hold something worthwhile and meaningful.

Life after loss won't ever be the same, we won't ever go back to the person we were, and when we're ready and willing, it's possible to find hope and meaning in life again.

Coping with a Lost Identity

After the death of a close family member or friend, some lose their sense of identity, self, or purpose. I grappled with that uncertainty after Miles's death. I felt lost. Empty. Confused. I didn't know who I was anymore or who I'd be in the world without him. But I knew I'd never be the same.

Being a mother to two sons and a bonus daughter through marriage was the greatest role that contributed to my sense of purpose. It gave my life fulfillment, joy, and meaning. My bond with each child is unique so the void that Miles's passing left couldn't be filled by anyone, not even my other son. Now that Miles was gone, I faced an unexpected crisis. I had lost my identity.

Who am I now that my loved one has passed? Am I still a parent, spouse, sibling?

Do I still have value or have anything to offer or give in life?

I sat at my desk and slowly read the email from a dear friend who shared how he struggled with identity after his wife died six years prior.

"I wrestled with the questions whether I, or we, were still a couple or not," Cedric wrote.

For those living with the death of a loved one, I'd learned grieving and coping with loss of identity wasn't uncommon. Our relationships with family, friends, and those with whom we regularly interact contribute significantly to our expression of who we are. When someone close to us dies, we often struggle with the change in those relational roles. For instance, we might be parents, spouses, children, family, friends, or caregivers, but after loss, we may feel unclear about who we are absent from that role.

During my struggle with identity and purpose after Miles transitioned, I agonized over hard questions.

How many children do I have now?

Do I still have two sons?

Would it be appropriate to say I have a son, Miles, although he's deceased?

I determined that being a mother was more than filling a role and performing duties. It embodies a relationship, bond, and love that brings life and meaning to motherhood. Those relational traits are unique and extend to each role we hold, and over time, I endeavored to find my place and Miles's place in my new reality. Death didn't take away my identity of being Miles's mother, but rather, reinforced that bond, keeping it alive.

I reconciled and determined how I'd present myself and my loss to the world. I was still a wife, mother, family member, friend, and even in his death, *remained* Miles's mother. The power lived within me to write my script regarding that identity.

When someone asks, "Do you have children?" I respond with, "I have two sons, but my younger son, Miles, passed away."

Whatever the role or relationship that connects us with our loved one, we can acknowledge and define who and what we'll be moving forward. That allows us to accept that we'll never be the person we were before the loss, and we can reshape our identity into one that affirms the purpose that binds us to our loved one. This act honors that relationship, validates the void that remains, and memorializes our loss.

What if I Can't Move Forward?

"My loved one is gone, I'll never be happy again," we tell ourselves.

Developing a desire to move forward without our loved one's physical presence often involves giving ourselves permission to reengage in life. That requires continuous work tailored to the needs of the grieving person.

At some point, most of us want to find hope in living, but we encounter obstacles that keep us from believing we can find joy in life again. Thoughts of betrayal and guilt leave us stagnant and depressed.

Some people say that if we seek to be happy after the death of someone close to us, we're minimizing the magnitude of our loss and that might imply we've moved beyond their deaths. Others think moving forward means we're betraying, forgetting, or leaving our beloveds in the past. I discovered that neither of those perceptions was true. When we attach our pain to staying connected and loyal to the person who died, we limit our ability to move beyond the place and time of loss.

I didn't know that I could live outside and alongside my loss. When I began my grief work, I discovered tools that inspired me to move forward. Our needs change with the experiences and seasons of our lives. For instance, at different times my work included receiving counseling, participating in grief classes, starting a support group for mothers of child loss, engaging in self-care, receiving emotional support from compassionate family and friends, and continually relying on my faith.

I found that moving forward and having a desire to enjoy life isn't betrayal, and it can be a pathway to honoring our loved ones. We honor them when we choose to carry them into the future and keep our relationship alive.

When we know we can embrace tears and laughter, memories and hopes, loss and life, the guilt of living lifts, and we find the desire to journey ahead. I accept moving forward is a decision I'll make each day for the rest of my life.

Still, the most powerful encouragement I received, which helped awaken the desire to live passionately and purposefully, comes from my son. On days when I believe I can't make it through another minute, I hear Miles's voice cheering me on.

"Mom, you can do this."

"I believe in you."

"That's *my* mom."

Knowing that my child is encouraging me to keep moving forward gives me courage to persevere and find meaning in life again.

When you close your eyes and listen to your heart's voice, what do you hear? The story we tell ourselves about moving forward will be used to fuel or suppress our ability to determine a future. Soon we learn that we can indeed find freedom and faith to move forward.

Moving Forward

Life after loss won't ever be the same, and we won't ever go back to the person we were. But when we're ready and willing, it's possible to find hope and meaning in life again.

YOU DON'T KNOW JUST HOW I FEEL

CHAPTER 15

Live Again

Every great loss demands that we choose life again. We need to grieve in order to do this. The pain we have not grieved over will always stand between us and life. When we don't grieve, a part of us becomes caught in the past like Lot's wife who, because she looked back, was turned into a pillar of salt.

—Rachel Naomi Remen

FOR MANY, FINDING THE will to live with expectancy demands patience to grieve fully and courage to believe life still has meaning. In the midst of mourning, life may seem unbearable and impossible.

The emotional, mental, and physical battles we fight during grief drain our confidence and we become insecure. Nothing can fill the agonizing hole left in our world, and we can't see a way out of our present state. We fear we don't have control over our future. These unsettling emotions strip us of the desire to expect anything more than a day-to-day existence. We take small steps toward reclaiming hope but lack momentum to maintain progress.

Once we determine and give ourselves a reason to participate in life, we can win those battles and begin to live again. I became hopeful when I found inspiration and motivation that propelled me forward. By releasing the agony and hopelessness of grief, I learned I *could* feel better and pursued my longing to live with perseverance and purpose.

I fought apprehension as I took steps forward and started participating in activities, engaging in hobbies, and socializing more. Sometimes I still wrestle with guilty feelings of Miles's not being alive to share my life, but those emotions don't overwhelm me as often or intensely as when I began my journey.

Finding the Will to Live

Like others, I've learned to redefine what happiness looks like in my life after loss. Many of our interests, experiences, and words have new meanings and significance. Our focus, goals, and priorities change as we find purpose and inspiration in new causes, build, strengthen, and purge relationships, and create meaningful ways to honor our loved ones. We change and adapt. Because of our loss, we accept that we're different, and life's different.

Through that acceptance, I realized if I chose to live without hope, happiness, or purpose, that representation wouldn't bring honor to Miles's life or his memory. I understood that life's a gift, and without hesitation I'd exchange mine, if it meant Miles could live. Knowing that, compels me to cherish Miles by living my life and embracing those things I'd hoped for his life: love, happiness, joy, and purpose. That's how I found peace and restored hope to live again.

Turning Pain into Purpose

Initially, I didn't want purpose to come from my grief. I only wanted my son. Yet I longed for a catalyst to which I could channel my pain and love for Miles that would ascribe something meaningful to his death. That didn't mean that I understood why, or believed Miles had to die in order for me to find this purpose, learn some greater lesson, or fulfill bigger tasks.

Rather, because he passed, I've chosen to do something meaningful to help myself and other hurting people find hope in spite of our suffering. Was I already doing this? Yes. But now I've chosen to expand that outreach to a larger community with those who grieve.

Each time I wrap my arms around a grieving mother, or someone who has experienced loss, I'm turning my pain into purpose. When I answer the phone or sit with someone who needs someone to listen to their story without judgment, I honor Miles's memory and carry his legacy forward.

Finding meaning is a personal act and no one else can find it for us. We shouldn't rush meaning or substitute it as an avenue of hurrying through grief or avoiding our pain. For most people that process takes time, often months, or even years after our loved one's transition. Meaning doesn't take away our pain, invalidate our loss, or equate to the cost of losing someone, but instead softens our grief by ascribing meaning to the way *we* live after our loved one dies.

LaSheita, my bonus daughter and Miles's sister, shared,

> Yes, losing a loved one hurts. One thing I've learned since Miles died, is his love didn't. The love I have for him is a living, breathing thing and that love helps me navigate to my new normal.
>
> Before Miles's death "love surpasses all things" was just another quote to me. Now, I know and understand its full meaning. Even in his death, my brother continues to touch my life. And for that, I am grateful.
>
> Yes, on some days my tears still flow. The difference now is that sometimes they are happy tears in remembrance of my beloved brother.

Since Miles's transition I've found meaning in starting a support group for mothers of child loss, establishing a memorial scholarship in his name, becoming a certified grief educator, and writing this book.

Whatever we choose to find meaning, doesn't have to be big or extraordinary, it only needs to be significant to us. There's great value in gratitude, meaningful moments, connections, and other ways we commemorate and honor our beloveds. Could finding meaning help ease your grief, make life more bearable, and enable you to move forward?

Integrating Grief

As we continue on our journey we find tools that help us sculpt our own path of comfort and healing. I became empowered to move forward when I learned that my grief needed to be *acknowledged*, *honored*, *heard*, *witnessed*, and *validated*.

Acknowledge. I learned to accept the truth about my grief soon after Miles's transition.

"How're you doing, Gwen?" family and friends asked.

"I'm hurting," I responded. Or I would say, "I'm having a tough day"; "I have bad days and I have okay days"; "I miss my child."

I didn't cover up with a customary, "I'm fine," so that others wouldn't feel uncomfortable. I knew I had to tell the truth about my pain and the power of that truth strengthened me in my grief.

Listen. At the onset of our bereavement, I repeated the story of the day my son transitioned.

"He'd just been upstairs with us."

"He went downstairs where he had a seizure."

I needed someone to hear my story of loss, and I told it a hundred times.

Those with whom I shared allowed me the time and space to be heard. This taught me how to be present with others in grief and the healing power of listening to the heart of those in deep pain. Helping others living with loss gives me a greater sense of purpose.

Honor and Meaning. When I talk about Miles and say his name, I show respect for his memory. Each meaningful action I pursue in his memory and to sustain his legacy softens the pain of his loss, inspiring me to move forward.

Witness and Validate. I give myself and others permission to address and observe our pain when I'm willing to sit with others in their darkest lamentations without judgment. I see them and share space with their grief.

Each time I talk about the reality of living with loss and give myself and others freedom to express emotions without judging or comparing our experiences to anyone else's, I attest to the truth of our circumstances and make room to mourn fully.

While the tools I've mentioned above can't erase the severity of my loss, they've enabled me to define and establish my personal norms and practices on my journey of healing.

Healing

Grief is complex, with many layers that impact our ability to move toward healing. Healing after loss is a day-to-day journey that continues for the rest of our lives. Those who resign themselves to a future filled with intense agony are surrendering to an unmerciful existence. There'll be times when living with grief is emotionally challenging and upsetting, but it doesn't have to become disabling.

Adjusting to loss is different for everyone and comparing our pain or how we grieve with anyone else's can be distressing; however, sharing and seeing ourselves in other people's stories can help us move forward as we identify paths to healing that others have traveled.

Reaching a place where we can begin healing from raw agony comes when we focus on our unique grief. Factors such as religious beliefs, relationships, life experiences, and personal needs influence how we approach life after loss. Whatever the circumstances, healing from grief can be a slow and demanding process.

A parent, whose child has passed, faces distinct challenges that differ from those of a surviving spouse, someone whose parent died, a sibling, another relative, or friend. The timing of the death can also affect healing. Was it sudden, unexpected, traumatic, or an extended illness?

Many yearn for closure regarding certain unresolved issues of their loss so they can focus on moving forward. Sometimes finding those answers, explanations, or other responses is critical in facilitating aspects of healing. Others think, *Someday I'll reach an end to my grief,* which is a misconception that they'll recover and revert to their old lives. Although we may long for resolution, some effects of grief remain with us. Each of us defines what healing feels and looks like in our own lives. We *can* begin to feel better and heal while emotionally, mentally, and physically acknowledging and validating our grief.

As we move forward, grief settles inside us, calms its distress, and integrates itself into our lives. That takes time and patience. Each of us decides when we're ready to move in that direction. Grief and happiness can occupy space within us simultaneously. We don't have to choose or deny either the opportunity to exist. Healing begins when we choose to remember our beloveds with more love and beautiful memories. There's hope in knowing that we can live our lives again.

Moving Forward

Each of us decides if and how we'll move forward. We determine what our own healing feels and looks like. Learning to embrace the integration of our emotional, mental, physical, and spiritual experiences challenges us to validate the complexity of our grief and healing. Grief and happiness can simultaneously occupy space within us. Acknowledging this relationship between emotions empowers us to live our truth while honoring the reality of our grief journeys.

Appendix

THIS APPENDIX IS A resource to help you on your grief journey. It contains the following:

"Scripture for Comfort and Encouragement" will encourage and strengthen you while you are adapting to and living with loss.

"Self-Care Tips during Grief" provides practical ways to incorporate emotional, mental, physical, and spiritual self-care practices into your day.

"Help Someone Who Is Grieving" offers general tips for helping people who have experienced loss and serves as a foundation for you to build on and formulate your own specific ways to help.

"Navigating Holidays and Other Milestone Events" will help you plan for and process these events.

Helpful Resources like websites and grief hotlines will help you while you are grieving.

Scriptures for Comfort and Encouragement in Loss

These Scriptures have comforted, encouraged, and strengthened me during times of loss. I wish the same for you as you move forward in hope and healing. (All Scripture is from the New International Version.)

So do not fear for I am with you; do not be dismayed, for I am your God. I will strengthen you and help you; I will uphold you with my righteous right hand (Isaiah 41:10).

He was despised and rejected by mankind, a man of suffering, and familiar with pain. Like one from whom people hide their faces he was despised, and we held him in low esteem (Isaiah 53:3).

The righteous perish, and no one takes it to heart; the devout are taken away, and no one understands that the righteous are taken away to be spared from evil. Those who walk uprightly enter into peace; they find rest as they lie in death (Isaiah 57:1–2).

You who are my Comforter in sorrow, my heart is faint within me (Jeremiah 8:18).

"For I know the plans I have for you," declares the LORD, "plans to prosper you and not to harm you, plans to give you hope and a future" (Jeremiah 29:11).

Though he brings grief, he will show compassion, so great is his unfailing love. For he does not willingly bring affliction or grief to anyone (Lamentations 3:32–33).

The LORD also will be a stronghold for the oppressed, a stronghold in times of trouble (Psalm 9:9).

Even though I walk through the darkest valley, I will fear no evil, for you are with me; your rod and your staff, they comfort me (Psalm 23:4).

Turn to me and be gracious to me, for I am lonely and afflicted (Psalm 25:16).

I remain confident in this: I will see the goodness of the LORD in the land of the living (Psalm 27:13).

Be merciful to me, LORD, for I am in distress; my eyes grow weak with sorrow, my soul and body with grief (Psalm 31:9).

The LORD is close to the brokenhearted and saves those who are crushed in spirit (Psalm 34:18).

God is our refuge and strength, a very present help in trouble (Psalm 46:1).

For this God is our God for ever and ever; he will be our guide even to the end (Psalm 48:14).

Though you have made me see troubles, many and bitter, you will restore my life again; from the depths of the earth you will again bring me up. You will increase my honor and comfort me once more (Psalm 71:20–21).

My flesh and my heart may fail, but God is the strength of my heart and my portion forever (Psalm 73:26).

Unless the LORD had given me help, I would soon have dwelt in the silence of death. When I said, "My foot is slipping," your unfailing love, LORD, supported me. When anxiety was great within me, your consolation brought me joy (Psalm 94:17–19).

May your unfailing love be my comfort, according to your promise to your servant (Psalm 119:76).

He heals the brokenhearted and binds up their wounds (Psalm 147:3).

Blessed are the poor in spirit, for theirs is the kingdom of heaven. Blessed are those who mourn, for they will be comforted (Matthew 5:3–4).

In the same way your Father in heaven is not willing that any of these little ones should perish (Matthew 18:14).

Jesus said, "Let the little children come to me, and do not hinder them, for the kingdom of heaven belongs to such as these" (Matthew 19:14).

And they can no longer die; for they are like the angels. They are God's children, since they are children of the resurrection (Luke 20:36).

For God so loved the world that he gave his one and only Son, that whoever believes in him shall not perish but have eternal life (John 3:16).

Jesus said to her, "I am the resurrection and the life. The one who believes in me will live, even though they die; and whoever lives by believing in me will never die. Do you believe this?" (John 11:25–26).

Do not let your hearts be troubled. You believe in God; believe also in me. My Father's house has many rooms; if that were not so, would I have told you that I am going there to prepare a place for you? (John 14:1–2).

Peace I leave with you; my peace I give you. I do not give to you as the world gives. Do not let your hearts be troubled and do not be afraid (John 14:27).

So with you: Now is your time of grief, but I will see you again and you will rejoice, and no one will take away your joy (John 16:22).

I have told you these things, so that in me you may have peace. In this world you will have trouble. But take heart! I have overcome the world (John 16:33).

I consider that our present sufferings are not worth comparing with the glory that will be revealed in us (Romans 8:18).

For I am convinced that neither death nor life, neither angels nor demons, neither the present nor the future, nor any powers, neither height nor depth, nor anything else in all creation, will be able to separate us from the love of God that is in Christ Jesus our Lord (Romans 8:38–39).

If we live, we live for the Lord; and if we die, we die for the Lord. So, whether we live or die, we belong to the Lord (Romans 14:8).

So will it be with the resurrection of the dead. The body that is sown is perishable, it is raised imperishable; it is sown in dishonor, it is raised in glory; it is sown in weakness, it is raised in power; and it is sown a natural body, it is raised a spiritual body. If there is a natural body, there is also a spiritual body (1 Corinthians 15:42–44).

O death, where is your victory? O death, where is your sting? (1 Corinthians 15:55).

Praise be to the God and Father of our Lord Jesus Christ, the Father of compassion and the God of all comfort, who comforts us in all our troubles, so that we can comfort those in any trouble with the comfort we ourselves receive from God. For just as we share abundantly in the sufferings of Christ, so also our comfort abounds through Christ (2 Corinthians 1:3–5).

For our light and momentary troubles are achieving for us an eternal glory that far outweighs them all. So we fix our eyes not on what is seen, but on what is unseen, since what is seen is temporary, but what is unseen is eternal (2 Corinthians 4:17–18).

We are confident, I say, and would prefer to be away from the body and at home with the Lord (2 Corinthians 5:8).

I have no one else like him, who will show genuine concern for your welfare (Philippians 2:20).

Brothers and sisters, we do not want you to be uninformed about those who sleep in death, so that you do not grieve like the rest of mankind, who have no hope. For we believe that Jesus died and rose again, and so we believe that God will bring with Jesus those who have fallen asleep in him (1 Thessalonians 4:13–14).

After that, we who are still alive and are left will be caught up together with them in the clouds to meet the Lord in the air. And so we will be with the Lord forever. Therefore encourage one another with these words (1 Thessalonians 4:17–18).

Dear friends, now we are children of God, and what we will be has not yet been made known. But we know that when Christ appears, we shall be like him, for we shall see him as he is (1 John 3:2).

Then I heard a voice from heaven say, "Write this: Blessed are the dead who die in the Lord from now on." "Yes," says the Spirit, "they will rest from their labor, for their deeds will follow them" (Revelation 14:13).

He will wipe every tear from their eyes. There will be no more death or mourning or crying or pain, for the old order of things has passed away (Revelation 21:4).

Self-Care Tips during Grief

These tips provide practical ways to incorporate emotional, mental, physical, and spiritual self-care practices into your day.

1. Be patient and compassionate with yourself.
2. Give yourself space and time to grieve fully.
3. Rest, sleep, and take breaks when you need to.
4. Eat healthy and drink water to help tend to your body.
5. Join a community, faith-based, or online support group.
6. Ask for help and be open to receive help from people in your support system.
7. Meet with a counselor and/or spiritual adviser who is experienced in dealing with loss.
8. Set and enforce boundaries where needed.
9. Read a book.
10. Keep a journal to release your thoughts and feelings.
11. Go for a walk or bike ride to connect with nature.
12. Exercise and move your body to release stress, tension, and pain.
13. Take a warm bath.
14. Breathe deeply and exhale.
15. Listen to music that comforts and soothes your soul.
16. Pray, meditate, and practice mindfulness.
17. Pets. Spending time with pets provides comfort and stress relief.
18. Be flexible and give yourself permission to change plans.
19. Avoid making major changes or decisions for at least one year.
20. Find meaningful ways to honor your loved one as you move forward.

Tips to Help Someone Who Is Grieving

These suggestions offer general tips for helping people who've experienced loss. It serves as a foundation for you to build on and formulate your own specific ways to help.

1. Remember there are no right or wrong ways to grieve.
2. Be *present* when you're with them. Be willing to sit with them and experience all of their emotions.
3. Silent. Sometimes when we don't know what to say being silent with them is enough.
4. Listen. Avoid giving unsolicited advice or trying to fix their pain.
5. Help. Offer specific ways to help, for example, picking up groceries, or children, or providing a meal.
6. Respect boundaries and don't be offended when there's a need to set or enforce them.
7. Don't offer platitudes or clichés.
8. Don't compare their grief with anyone else's.
9. Keep the focus on them, their grief and loss, not on you.
10. Don't ask details about how their loved one died or other traumatic topics.
11. Say their loved one's name or share uplifting stories about them.
12. Don't judge or rush. Allow them to move forward at their own pace and time. There's no timetable for grief.
13. Call, text, email, send a note or card, with a simple message like, "Thinking of you," that doesn't require the receiver to respond.
14. Continue to support and keep in contact beyond the initial days, weeks, or months after loss.
15. Be aware of warning signs that they may need additional help.

Tips for Navigating Holidays and Other Milestone Events

Navigating holidays and other milestone days and events is challenging. It's not important what you choose to do, but that you remember them and honor any emotions that you might experience.

1. Rest and be gentle with yourself.
2. Don't feel pressured to do anything you don't want to do.
3. Cry if you need to.
4. Allow others to help and provide support.
5. Don't forget about others, like children, who may also need support.
6. Make time to be alone.
7. Give yourself time and space to process emotions.
8. Don't feel guilty about saying no or declining invitations.
9. Don't feel guilty about saying yes or accepting invitations.
10. Honor your loved one's favorite holiday traditions.
11. Begin new traditions.
12. Include your loved one in celebrations by sharing a story about them.
13. Light a candle in honor of your loved one.
14. Create a tribute.
15. Do something they loved to do.
16. Spend time with family and friends.
17. Make a donation in their name.
18. Confide in a trusted friend, counselor, or spiritual adviser if you're hurting deeply or feeling overwhelmed.
19. Don't place emotional expectations or anticipations around how the day or event will be, but choose to allow it to unfold on its own.
20. Rely on your faith and religious beliefs for comfort.

Helpful Resources

Crisis Hotlines, Websites, and Grief Support

If you are suicidal or in crisis, please call one of the Crisis Hotlines immediately.

Call 1-800-273-8255. You are not alone. Help is on the way.

Crisis Hotlines

Immediate Danger. Call 911.

National Suicide Prevention Hotline. 1-800-273-8255. This number is toll free, 24 hours a day, 7 days a week.

Websites: www.SuicideHotlines.com

www.suicidepreventionlifeline.org.

Phone: 1-800-273-TALK

1-800-273-8255

1-800-799-4889 (for hearing impaired).

Grief Support

The Compassionate Friends. Supporting family after a child dies.

Website: www.compassionatefriends.org.

Phone: 1-877-969-0010

1-630-990-0010

Grief.com. Grief.com is an online resource and support center established by David Kessler, the world's foremost expert on grief and loss.

Website: www.Grief.com.

GriefShare. GriefShare is a faith-based program with local groups throughout the United States and internationally for people grieving the death of a family member or friend.

Website: www.griefshare.org.

Phone: 1-800-395-5755 (US and Canada)

1-919-562-2112 (International)

Monday–Friday, 9:00 a.m. to 5:00 p.m. EST

Bibliography

Altura, Mayo Clinic affiliate. "20 Ways to Take Care of Yourself while Grieving," Aug. 2, 2019. https://www.altru.org/blog/2019/august/20-ways-to-take-care-of-yourself-while-grieving/.

Brown, Brené. *Daring Greatly: How the Courage to Be Vulnerable Transforms the Way We Live, Love, Parent, and Lead.* New York: Avery Publishers, 2015.

Cloud, Dr. Henry and Dr. John Townsend. *Boundaries, Updated and Expanded Edition: When to Say Yes, How to Say No to Take Control of Your Life.* Grand Rapids, MI: Zondervan, 2017.

Devine, Megan. *It's OK That You're Not Okay: Meeting Grief and Loss in a Culture That Doesn't Understand.* Louisville, CO: Sounds True Publishers, 2017.

Devine, Megan. "What Is Grief Shaming?" YouTube video clip for the documentary, *Speaking Grief,* https://www.youtube.com/watch?v=QSCXyYuT2rE.

Earnshaw, Elizabeth, LMFT, CGT. *I Want This to Work: An Inclusive Guide to Navigating the Most Difficult Relationship Issues We Face in the Modern Age.* Louisville, CO: Sounds True Publishers, 2021.

Glover Tawwab, Nedra. *Setting Boundaries, Finding Peace: A Guide to Reclaiming Yourself.* New York: TarcherPerigee, an imprint of Penguin Random House, 2021.

Haley, Eleanor. "We Don't Recover from Grief and that's Okay," *What's Your Grief?* Podcast, April 3, 2019. https://whatsyourgrief.com/grief-recovery-is-not-a-thing/.

Kessler, David. *Finding Meaning: The Sixth Stage of Grief.* New York: Simon & Schuster, 2019.

Kessler, David. www.grief.com.

Kessler, David. https://www.davidkesslertraining.com/selfcare.

Kübler-Ross, Elisabeth, and David Kessler. *On Grief and Grieving: Finding the Meaning of Grief through the Five Stages of Loss.* New York: Scribner, 2005.

Lifton, Robert Jay. *Thought Reform and the Psychology of Totalism: A Study of "Brainwashing" in China,* New York: W. W. Norton & Co., 1961.

Mayo Clinic, online blog. "Grief: Coping with Reminders after a Loss," https://www.mayoclinic.org/healthy-lifestyle/end-of-life/in-depth/grief/art-20045340.

Mendoza, Marilyn A. PhD. "When Grief Gets Physical: Our Bodies and Mourning," *Psychology Today*, posted September 4, 2019. https://www.psychologytoday.com/us/blog/understanding-grief/201909/when-grief-gets-physical.

Seaburn, David B., PhD., LMFT. "Guilt, Helplessness, and a Path Forward," *Psychology Today*, posted February 3, 2020. https://www.psychologytoday.com/us/blog/going-out-not-knowing/202002/guilt-helplessness-and-path-forward.

van der Kolk, Bessell. *The Body Keeps the Score: Brain, Mind, and Body in the Healing of Trauma.* New York: Penguin Publishing Group, 2014.

Wolfelt, Alan D., Ph.D. *Understanding Your Grief: Ten Essential Touchstones for Finding Hope and Healing Your Heart,* XX: Companion Press, 2004.

Zuba, Tom. *Becoming Radiant.* Rockford, IL: Bish Press, 2018.

Zuba, Tom. *Permission to Mourn: A New Way to Do Grief.* Rockford, IL: Bish Press, 2014.

Acknowledgments

LIVING WITH THE DEATH of a child is one of the most difficult and painful experiences I have endured, and writing this book about that grief has been the hardest assignment and labor of love God has given me. I have not been on this journey alone. He also gave me people who walked beside me, encouraged me, prayed for me, and helped me bring this labor of love to publication. Words cannot express the abundance of love and support you've showered on me. I offer my sincere thanks to you and to God for putting you in my life.

To my husband, Robert, "Bob," words are inadequate to express the journey we've shared in life and loss. Thank you for always supporting and believing in me and giving me the time and space and for your encouragement and love that strengthened me.

My son, RL, you're a compassionate, kind, and loving king of a man. You've endured much in your life, yet your confidence, resilient spirit and faith continues to inspire and encourage others. Thanks for stopping whatever you were doing to pray for me and for continuously telling me, "Mom, you can do this." You are indeed the keeper of your brother's heart and the light that shines brightly in the dark places of life for others. You're my pride and joy. I pray God continues to heal your gentle heart.

To my brother, Alvin, and sister-in-love, Carol Odoms, and nieces Kendria Odoms Jones and Ashley Odoms. When Miles transitioned you began walking with and encouraging me on my grief journey, only to experience the loss of your beloved son and brother, my nephew,

AJ, four years later during the time I'd begun writing this book. Our hearts are forever knitted together as we navigate our journeys. Our love, encouragement, and support for one another remains strong as each day we move forward with hope and healing. Together we will make it through.

Jeneil Magloire, my sister-friend of thirty years, I'm blessed to have you walk beside me on life's journey. Thank you for your consistent support and for helping me push through the difficult days, encouraging me to take a break when I needed to, and knowing just what to say when I needed to hear it. I thank God for you, my friend.

My bonus daughters, LaSheita Clemons, thanks for checking in and sharing your heart about your brother, Miles, and to Alexandria Gignac, your daily check-ins and status inquiries meant so much and kept me going. Thank you both for your love and support. I love you.

Stephanie DeVeaux, you called me and asked, "Are you writing a book? God said you're supposed to write a book." Then you proceeded to get me started on the journey to writing this book. My dear friend, thank you for confirming God's assignment to me and being with me at every stage of this process. I'm thankful for you.

Pastor Anitha Jones, my pastor and spiritual life coach, mentor, and friend, thank you for showing me from your book how to cooperate with my season and how to press *Beyond Your Breakdown to Your Breakthrough*. Thanks for your prayers, leadership, encouragement, and example. Our family is blessed to have you and Pastor Tom Jones as our spiritual parents.

Cecil Murphey, my mentor, writing coach, and friend. I am honored to be your protégé. Thank you for teaching me the craft of writing so that this message of hope can reach the world. I thank God for you. You are a blessing to the world.

Donna Johnson, my Colorado mom, your love and encouragement means more than you can ever know. Thank you for adopting my family as your own. I love you dearly.

Jason Robinson, my personal trainer and "Lil/Big" brother, who helped me revive my love of the sport of physical fitness after Miles died.

From the first day I committed to writing this book, you believed in the vision and cheered me on. Thanks for always pushing me to aim for the impossible and to become the best version of myself.

To my FHG ministry family, thank you for your unfailing love, prayers, and support. You're amazing.

My Sisters in Solace support group, mothers of child loss, thank you for your love and support. May you find comfort in the pages of this book.

Thank you to everyone who allowed me to share their grief stories. I pray that your transparency will help to bring enlightenment, healing, and hope to others.

To the many family members and friends who encouraged and prayed for me while I wrote this book, and to my Colorado and Alabama support teams, thanks for bringing me food, getting me out to exercise, and encouraging me to take a break. You're the best.

My fellow Proteges, I'm blessed to be on this journey with you. Thanks for encouraging and praying me through the writing process. I appreciate you.

To the dynamic team of professionals at Redemption Press Publishers, and to my editor, Tisha Martin, thank you for ensuring that the message I share with the world is done so with excellence.

Wanda Rosenberry, thank you for editing the initial draft of my manuscript. Your work is commendable.

To Crimson, Prada, and Parker, who are more than doggies but family members who walked beside me and my family and provided comfort, support, and unconditional love as we navigated our grief journeys.

ORDER INFORMATION

To order additional copies of this book, please visit
www.redemption-press.com.
Also available at Christian bookstores and Barnes and Noble.